Living in
MEXICO
A Complete Guide

Michael Zamba

Printed on recyclable paper

PASSPORT BOOKS
a division of *NTC Publishing Group*
Lincolnwood, Illinois USA

Dedication

▼▼

To the person who introduced me to Mexico and its people, and all the people who continue to stimulate my fascination with this great country.

1995 Printing

Published by Passport Books, a division of NTC Publishing Group,
©1991 by NTC Publishing Group, 4255 West Touhy Avenue,
Lincolnwood (Chicago), Illinois 60646-1975 U.S.A.
Library of Congress Catalog Card Number: 90-61715
Manufactured in the United States of America.

4 5 6 7 8 9 VP 9 8 7 6 5 4 3

Contents

▼▼

Acknowledgments

▼▼▼

Although one name appears on the cover of this book, the work and guidance of many individuals has made *Living in Mexico* possible.

Following are a few of the people who have been instrumental in this book: Rebecca Robles, who introduced the writer to Mexico's wonders and was supportive during the publishing of *Living in Mexico;* María F. Pinzón, who spent countless hours proofing the manuscript and offering support; Eduardo Saenz, who introduced the author to the topic of retirement in Mexico; Margaret Newman for providing logistical support; Luz María Fernández for her help; and Lucila Horta Ruiz for her support; Lloyd Wilkins, publisher of *AIM, Adventures in Mexico,* for providing reliable background on important cities; and Robert Paral, who introduced the author to Passport Books.

Several hotel representatives made their time and services available to the author: Carlos E. Reyes, Marketing Director, Stouffer El Presidente in Mexico City; Lourdes García-Mora, Public Relations Director, Stouffer El Presidente in Mexico City; Suzanne Lewis, Sales Manager, El Tapatío Hotel in Guadalajara; and Jorg Neuehaus, General Manager, Westin Camino Real in Mexico City.

Retirees in Mexico made their opinions available, and I would like to extend my appreciation to them. Most of all, I extend my congratulations to all the people who are calling Mexico home either full or part-time. For retirees on their way to Mexico, I say: ¡Bienvenidos a México!

Michael J. Zamba

Foreword

▼▼

Living in or visiting Mexico is a very personal experience. For this writer, who has traveled to Europe, Canada, and across the United States, living in Mexico has brought a new view of the world. Mexico is a country that gets into your heart and continues to pull at it after you leave the country.

Residing in Mexico is unique because you are surrounded by people and a nation that are growing into the twenty-first century, while maintaining the architectural wonders and cultural romance of centuries past. One of the goals of *Living in Mexico* is to capture this sense by blending history with modern life.

Living in Mexico contains more information on Mexican history than is probably expected by readers. A retiree living in Chapala made a recommendation for potential new residents: "Mexicans know more about you than you know about them. Mexicans are rich in culture, and they are proud of it. If you are coming down, I would recommend you learn more about the country."

The purpose of this book is not to sell Mexico as a retirement spot; rather, it is a guide to the nation. It seeks to provide a glimpse of areas that retirees should consider and offer a way of looking at Mexico and living in the country.

Living in Mexico examines ten cities that are popular with foreign retirees, including Guadalajara, Cuernavaca, and San Miguel de Allende. Retirees have moved to other Mexican cities, such as Morelia and Oaxaca, but their numbers are relatively few. The book does not include reviews of these cities, however, since they do not have a large number of retirees. These communities have their appeal and are wonderful to see, but they may not be what most would-be residents are seeking.

Americans

It must be noted that there is a difference between an American and a person from the United States. People from throughout this hemisphere are considered Americans, not just those individuals from the United States. This book, however, uses the term to describe people from the United States, since it has become a common reference in this country.

Finally, prices for housing and the like are estimations only; each person will find that costs vary. Also, telephone numbers for golf courses, hotels, and other businesses listed in this book are subject to change.

Buena suerte, which means "Good luck."

1

To Retire in Paradise

S itting in an open-air café off San Miguel de Allende's *zócalo,* a 55-year-old American writer was sipping coffee and talking about his move from Los Angeles, California, eight months earlier. "Los Angeles was getting too distracting and expensive, so it was time for a change," he said.

He set down his cup of coffee and pointed across the street to the *zócalo,* which is a typical Mexican central plaza where people converge for afternoon gatherings or relaxation.

"It's obvious," he said, as we looked at the people enjoying a sunny afternoon in the tree-encircled plaza, "life could never have been this good to me in Los Angeles; I have plenty of time to write, relax, and visit the country. I've made new friends, and I keep prodding my old friends from the States to come down."

1

San Miguel de Allende, the second largest city in the state of Guanajuato and situated some four hours from Mexico City, is known for its tranquil atmosphere, colonial setting, and home-grown art school. It is also known for the ten thousand Americans who live in harmony with approximately fifty thousand Mexican citizens.

It was more than the calm atmosphere that drew the Southern Californian to this colonial city. He had heard about a writing school in San Miguel de Allende and a large American community that was living more comfortably there than in most of the suburbs of Los Angeles.

Quality of Life

▼▼▼▼▼▼▼▼▼▼▼▼▼▼▼▼▼▼▼▼▼▼▼▼▼▼▼▼▼▼▼▼▼▼▼▼▼

Mexico has long been a magnet for a variety of people—gold and silver miners, adventurers, moviemakers, business representatives, and tourists. The rich and famous, from actress Helen Hayes to the late director John Huston, have called Mexico home.

But Mexico is not only for the rich or the adventuresome. Thousands of American, Canadian, and British citizens are moving to Mexico to enjoy their golden years in a place they call paradise. In fact, some 250,000 English-speaking retirees have said *adiós* to Florida, Southern California, and other Sunbelt retreats and *hola* to Mexico. The U.S. State Department estimates that nearly 400,000 Americans have taken up full- and part-time residence in Mexico—flocking to beachfront condominiums, colonial towns, and thriving retirement communities.

▲▲

U.S. Citizens in Mexico
for Selected Cities

Guadalajara	42,000
Juárez	28,600
Mexico City	255,600
Monterrey	9,000
Tijuana	42,000

Source: Unpublished fiscal year 1988 statistics, U.S. State Department, Office of Overseas Citizenship Services.

There are many reasons for living in Mexico, but you could easily fit them under the general heading of "Quality of Life." Let us examine some of the strongest magnets that have drawn Americans to Mexico.

Climate

In Neil Simon's movie *California Suite,* a man was asked to explain why he moved from New York City to Southern California. He said it was simple. When it is 90 degrees in August in New York, it is 70 degrees in Southern California. When it is 10 degrees and snowing in New York, it is 70 degrees in Southern California. The same can be said of most places in Mexico.

Guadalajara, Jalisco, is the best-known retirement area in Mexico. When asked why a person moves to *La perla del occidente,* (the Pearl of the West) almost every resident automatically gives one reason—climate.

3

While *best* is a relative term, Guadalajara boasts of a year-round daytime temperature in the mid to upper 70 degrees. Indeed, the rainy season in Guadalajara, which runs from June to the beginning of October, is considered the best time for the city because the late-night showers clear the air and morning rushes in with clear skies and a mild temperature that climbs to roughly 79 degrees.

Mexico is fortunate. It does not have a winter as in U.S. midwestern or northern states, where snow piles up on the driveway and anyone who ventures outdoors must dress in layers of wool, and other fabrics to stay warm. Mexico has a variety of climates: from the hot and humid resort area of Cancún on the Yucatán Peninsula, to the relatively cool and dry city of Cuernavaca about one hour from Mexico City. Individual chapters in this book will examine differences in climate among the cities, but it is safe to say that leaving Chicago, Detroit, New York, or Boston—even Miami or Los Angeles—will provide the new resident with a steady climate to enjoy.

Price

Mexico is definitely inexpensive. Mexico has been devaluating its currency, the peso, against the U.S. dollar almost daily since the early 1980s. These economic adjustments have been extremely favorable to people with foreign currency— especially U.S. dollars. The *verde* (green) can go very far in Mexico (some merchants prefer the dollar over the peso), and the strength of the dollar gives Americans an enormous edge against inflation.

The government fixes the price of most food sold in markets, such as milk, corn, beans, and other staples. Official price increases are fairly infrequent, much to the pleasure of the consumer and disdain of the producer. For example, a

4

liter of milk in May 1990 cost 2,000 pesos, or less than one U.S. dollar; and a kilo of beans was priced at 3,800 pesos, which is about $1.50. For people who desire them, U.S.-made products—including home appliances, certain foods, and even beer—are showing up on Mexican shelves, and that trend is expected to continue as both countries work to reduce trade barriers.

How much can a person live on in Mexico? It depends on the person's lifestyle. Some books and articles boast that people can live comfortably in Mexico on as little as $400 a month, including a home, food, and light entertainment. Realistically, residents say to expect your costs to be from $500 to $1,000 a month; however, that range includes good housing, fresh food, maid service, a cook, entertainment, and other activities. "Find that kind of lifestyle on a retiree's income in the United States," one resident challenges.

Convenience

Travel from the United States to Mexico is fairly simple. More than 450 airline flights each week connect the neighbors.

Guadalajara, Mexico City, Acapulco, and Puerto Vallarta are just a few of the popular cities with international, nonstop flights from the United States. Flights and fares to Mexico from locations such as Chicago, New York, Baltimore, and a few other major northern cities are comparable to those for destinations in Florida, Arizona, and Southern California.

Driving to Mexico can also be a likely option. The condition of Mexico's roads varies, based on their popularity and location, with some roads being nothing more than loosely spread gravel over a tire-beaten dirt track and others being smooth multilane superhighways. In 1989, Mexico's Ministry of Tourism announced that the government would work aggressively during the next six years to enhance roadways that are popular with tourists. Driving to Mexico and traveling within the country with your car or by alternative domestic transportation are discussed in a later chapter.

People

The first thing you will notice about the Mexican people are the children. Their big brown eyes, dark hair, and tan skin are an instant attraction for both visitors and residents. The children scamper up to people, asking them questions and offering to help them or to accompany them down the street. The children are rarely a bother, however, and their company is usually enjoyable.

Mexicans are probably the nicest people you can encounter. While their houses are surrounded by walls, their hearts are not. They open their homes to guests, offer coffee and pastries, and chat with newcomers. Mexicans are very proud of their country, and most take any opportunity to show it off to visitors.

On the whole, Mexicans genuinely like the *gringos* who live there. They are fascinated by the United States as a country and will typically quiz all visitors on a wide variety of subjects. Likewise, the retirees have generally befriended the Mexicans. Some retiree organizations even have set up scholarship funds for Mexicans, and in some cities they share library facilities and celebrate holidays together.

Snowbirds vs. Full-time Residents

▼▼▼

Two types of Americans live in Mexico—snowbirds and the full-time residents.

A snowbird is like a migrating duck from the north. When the weather in Chicago, Detroit, New York, and elsewhere starts to turn messy around October or November, a large number of retired snowbirds pack up their belongings and move south. Even some people who live in the U.S. Sunbelt seek refuge in Mexico when their communities become popular wintering grounds for other retirees. In Mexico, these seasonal residents enjoy a comfortable climate while the people back home shiver through the cold winter months.

All the major cities receive an influx of migrating snowbirds, whose presence is always welcome. Many snowbirds have businesses or family responsibilities that prevent them from living in Mexico yearlong. Others simply enjoy getting away from the chilly weather, the snowdrifts, and the ice for a few months.

Many retirees prefer the stability and continuity of lifestyle that come with being full-time residents. Full-time residents who own their house or apartment in Mexico do not need to worry about renting it during the off seasons or having it looked after by a management company. Also, hired help, such as maids or gardeners, can be retained all year. In addition, full-time residents can take advantage of the varied course offerings of the local educational programs.

Deciding on how long to live in Mexico is personal. Considerations at home, such as managing a business or attending to family needs, have to be weighed against full-time retirement. Being a snowbird offers the best of both worlds— a stable summer in the north and a sunny winter in the south.

The length of time spent in Mexico varies from person to person; some people start off as snowbirds and eventually become full-time residents.

Will I Like It?

▼▼

Can this experience be for me? Every person must make this decision. "One thing is certain, foreign retirees can live nicely in Mexico for far less than they spend in the United States, with ideal climates to boot," says Bob Wilson, publisher of a newsletter on retirement in Mexico. "Over and over again, we urge potential retirees to take a hard look at Mexico for themselves. No retirement spot in the world can suit everybody."

All residents are candid on one point: Mexico may not be for everyone, but neither is Florida nor California nor a host of other places throughout the world. Some people have tried it and left. Most, however, become embraced in the arms of Mexico and have warm feelings for its people.

Many Americans who choose to live in Mexico still maintain many of their social activities. As Mexico's popularity as a retirement location grows, chapters of U.S. organizations, including the Veterans of Foreign Wars and even Alcoholics Anonymous, have been established and are running. New social organizations specifically for U.S. retirees in Mexico have been created, such as the Friends of Acapulco, and they continue to draw new members. Other informal, but regular, activities are arranged; for example, former New Yorkers now living in Guadalajara hold monthly meetings.

Besides the club events, residents keep busy throughout the day by shopping for handmade products, traveling to new cities, and going to school, among many other activities. For golfing enthusiasts, fantastic golf courses throughout the

8

country have been designed by some of the top golfing professionals, and the greens fees are inexpensive when compared to U.S. prices. For tennis buffs, most popular retirement cities have public and private tennis courts that retirees can utilize. There is almost always something to do for people with all kinds of interests.

Certainly Americans can live separate lives from the Mexicans, but most retirees have decided to live alongside and among their new neighbors. By slowly breaking down language and cultural barriers, each group finds out how truly fascinating the other really is. Without question, Mexico can provide its new residents with memorable, personal experiences.

The best advice any friend can offer is to find out as much as you can about the country through reading and travel. Fortunately, a trip to scout the highlights of Mexico is relatively inexpensive, with off-season visits affording the best opportunities to examine some of the major retirement locations. Guadalajara, Chapala, and Ajijic are within driving distance of each other and can be explored during a weekend. Puerto Vallarta is only a four-hour bus ride from Guadalajara.

Before and during your visits to Mexico, contact organizations and people who can answer your questions and assist you in your explorations. You will find a listing of helpful organizations in chapter 9.

Your First Step Toward Living in Mexico

▼▼▼▼▼▼▼▼▼▼▼▼▼▼▼▼▼▼▼▼▼▼▼▼▼▼▼▼▼▼▼▼▼▼▼▼▼▼

Mexico has something to offer every visitor and resident, including a stable climate, refreshing natural spas, outdoor activities, and an affordable lifestyle. Moving from the United

States or Canada to Mexico is much easier than a person suspects, and settling down south of the border can be rewarding.

Mexico is contagious. Without your knowing, the country and its people sneak up on you and steal your heart. This guidebook offers valuable information on Mexico, but reading is not enough. You must visit Mexico before you make any decisions. As the slogan says, "Come. Feel the warmth of Mexico!"

2

Mexico and You

T he alluring prospect of Mexico's warm climate, wonderful people, and good lifestyle on a reasonable budget has captured your imagination. The books and articles you have read about retiring in Mexico have made it sound easy to live south of the border.

So now what do you do? Do you pack your belongings, sell the house, say good-bye to your neighbors, and grab the first flight to Guadalajara? Definitely not! First you must ask yourself some serious questions before your exploratory visits and then be prepared to answer them candidly while you are there.

Some Personal Considerations

▼▼▼▼▼▼▼▼▼▼▼▼▼▼▼▼▼▼▼▼▼▼▼▼▼▼▼▼▼▼▼▼▼▼▼▼▼▼

Can I live outside the United States?

You may have had an opportunity to travel to other countries and see how they differ from the United States. If you have not visited other nations, there are several important things to remember.

Mexico is not the United States. The culture and language are different. If you relish living in your computerized, electronic home environment; if you cannot accept or appreciate people whose values differ from yours; and if you cringe at the suggestion of a change in your routine; then Mexico may not be the paradise you seek.

On the other hand, if you are not wed to the most recent appliances and conveniences, if you are flexible and open to new experiences, and if you are respectful of different values and ways of life, than Mexico may be right for you.

Certainly there are too many differences—both abstract and practical—between Mexico and the United States to list them here. One noticeable difference, however, is that far fewer modern conveniences are available in Mexico than in the United States. Dishwashers, garbage disposals, washers and dryers are not readily available in Mexico because they are expensive. This is not the end of the world. Middle- and upper-class Mexicans have accommodated themselves by hiring people to help out in their homes. Like the Mexicans, retirees have found domestic help to be a way to make up for these mechanical "shortcomings."

What do I expect to find in Mexico?

Images of Mexico abound. Some people have the idea that life in Mexico is like *The Treasure of the Sierra Madre,* in which Humphrey Bogart and Walter Huston sought riches in the wild Mexican mountains. Other people imagine Mexico to be like the brochures that show off the beaches, the happy faces of children, and the many archeological wonders. These are all images of Mexico. Since Mexico is a diverse nation of more than 80 million people, it offers more than a person can explore in a lifetime.

How inexpensively, or lavishly, do I want to live?

Mexico offers a range of price opportunities, from bare bones to extreme opulence. A realistic budget, with a reliable source of non-Mexican income, is essential to a successful life in Mexico.

An average couple of Americans living in Ajijic mentioned that numerous retirees have traveled to the Lake Chapala area expecting to live on $300 to $400 a month. Although a few people may be able to live comfortably on that income, the typical U.S. retiree would probably want a higher standard of living.

An average couple with a reasonable lifestyle should expect to spend $500 to $1,000 a month on all expenses, including a home, food, maid service, entertainment, and travel. At this level of income, retirees can enjoy life in Mexico as happily as they probably envisioned it.

Some Practical Considerations

▼▼▼▼▼▼▼▼▼▼▼▼▼▼▼▼▼▼▼▼▼▼▼▼▼▼▼▼▼▼▼▼▼▼▼▼▼

No entiendo: Learning the Language

No entiendo means "I don't understand" in Spanish. One of the toughest questions to answer is whether it is necessary to learn the language.

Spanish is the official language of Mexico and is used in all government activities. Although many Mexicans (particularly people with college degrees and others who deal with tourists) have a general understanding of English, retirees say it is a good idea to obtain a basic understanding of simple Spanish. Being able to ask simple questions, such as "Where is the restaurant?" *(¿Dónde está el restaurante?)* or "How much does this cost?" *(¿Cuánto cuesta?)* will not only make life a little easier but also will foster goodwill with your Mexican neighbors.

You will not be isolated by a lack of Spanish, however. English-language newspapers are circulated throughout the nation, including numerous weeklies and Mexico City's daily *The News,* as well as imported U.S. newspapers and magazines, such as *USA Today,* the *New York Times,* and *Time.* U.S. television networks are broadcast courtesy of cable television, which is available in areas that are popular with retirees. English-language books are also available: San Miguel de Allende, for example, has the largest bilingual library in the nation, and other retirement areas have more than adequate libraries.

Enrolling in Spanish-language classes in Mexico is fairly easy and courses are widely available. Many different programs are offered at schools and through retiree organizations. In fact, many language teachers agree that learning the language once you are in the country is much easier than learning it at home in the United States. Teachers say that because you are reminded of the language and customs daily, your lessons are more likely to take hold. Also, language classes in Mexico can be less expensive than classes in the United States.

Learning Spanish has more than just practical applications. Learning the language opens doors to a rich cultural heritage and provides insight into the humor and soul of the people. In the end, learning a language can be fun and a great way to meet people in your adopted country.

Immigration

U.S. citizens are permitted to travel in Mexico as long as they have proof of their nationality and a valid visa. Proof of U.S. citizenship can be demonstrated through various means, such as one of following:

- A U.S. birth certificate: This must be an original that has a raised official seal; photocopies will not do.

- An original U.S. naturalization certificate: Photocopies are not acceptable, and the U.S. government does not permit it.

- A U.S. voter registration card and a photo ID.

- A valid U.S. passport, which is issued by the U.S. State Department's Passport Services Office.

Of these documents, the U.S. passport is the best because it can be registered with the U.S. embassy and replaced if it is lost. In addition, the passport can be used when cashing traveler's checks and at other times when a photo identification is needed.

Mexican Visas

A visa is needed to live in or visit Mexico. The only exception is for travel within a short distance of the U.S.-Mexican border, which includes towns such as Tijuana, Ciudad Juárez, and Nuevo Laredo.

There are different types of visas, and each one offers certain benefits for retirees.

Tourist visas are the simplest to obtain and probably the most prevalent among retirees. Tourist visas are issued for periods of up to 180 days—often without question—and permit a visitor to roam the country. A tourist visa, technically called the FM-T, does not require any proof of income and can be filled out quickly without legal help. If a retiree is not planning to work for pay in Mexico, the tourist visa may be the best option for casual stays.

Many snowbird retirees obtain a tourist visa at the time they enter the country. At the conclusion of 180 days, they simply cross the border and then return to Mexico with a new visa. The visa should be kept in a safe place because the holder is required to turn it in when leaving the country. If you plan to travel any distance from your Mexican home, the visa should be in your possession.

If you enter Mexico by car, mobile home, or other personal vehicle, you must declare it on the visa. Tourists who enter in their personal vehicles must also leave with them. Mexico does not want Americans driving their cars across the border, only to sell or leave them. If your vehicle becomes lost, stolen, or unable to leave with the visitor, you will need government certification of the fact.

Visitante Rentista allows immigrants to have legal residence for up to two years. Technically called the FM-3, this visa does not permit the holder to work.

The FM-3 visa is reserved for people age 55 years or older. A younger person may obtain the the FM-3 if his or her spouse meets the age requirements. Since it is not a work permit, the government reasons that people older than age 55 are unlikely to seek employment. The FM-3 visa permits the holder to stay in Mexico for up to two years without having to leave. There is a renewal fee every six months. Applicants will need to provide the following:

- Proof of income: $1,000 a month for each cardholder, and $500 a month for each dependent. For Social Security recipients, a letter from the U.S. embassy will suffice. Retirees living on other sources of income, such as investments, will need a notarized letter from the bank and proof of deposits. Letters from a U.S. bank must be translated into Spanish and certified by the nearest Mexican consul (see listing in chapter 9).

- Letter of request: This letter can be prepared for free at the *Delegación de Servicios Migratorios,* which is the immigration service.

- Tourist visa: The original plus two photocopies must be submitted.

- Passport: A notarized photocopy of your passport.

- Letter: A letter to verify your current address must be in Spanish and signed by two people who know you.

- Documents: Marriage and birth certificates must be translated into Spanish and certified by the nearest Mexican consul.

- Medical exam: You must obtain a letter from a Mexican doctor that confirms you are in good health and that you are not carrying any communicable diseases.

- Photographs: Several passport-type photographs must be submitted with the application.

Retirees have obtained the FM-3 visa without a lawyer, but many people recommend seeking the help of a qualified attorney. The U.S. embassy and local retiree organizations may offer the names of good lawyers in your Mexican city. If no list is available in your area, interview a few English-speaking attorneys to find out how many FM-3 visas they have processed and the average time it takes before their clients receive their card.

Inmigrante Rentista, which is also available for retirees, provides for greater privileges. Like the FM-3 visa, the *Inmigrante Rentista* is issued to people age 50 years and older and does not permit the holder to work. This visa, referred to technically as an FM-2, allows holders to bring in a wide variety of personal property, including all household goods for an average home. It also allows the holder to apply for *Inmigrado* status within five years (see below).

FM-2 holders can bring in their own U.S.-made automobile and leave the country without it. At the end of five years, however, the car must be brought back and left in the United States. If approved for FM-2 status, retirees are given a passportlike booklet in which their border crossings are recorded. The holders must pay a renewal fee every six months.

Applying for an FM-2 visa will require the same actions as listed for an FM-3 visa, as well as a letter of good conduct issued by the local police in the United States. As with other documents, this letter must be translated into Spanish and certified by the nearest Mexican consul.

Inmigrado status gives a resident all the privileges of Mexican citizenship, with the exception of voting rights. Chief among the benefits are the ability to work and own a business and the opportunity to bring in more of their own belongings from the United States.

Mexican immigration laws can be quite cumbersome, and wading through the bureaucratic red tape can be a frustrating experience. Much of the work, however, can be handled at government offices in major cities like Guadalajara or Cuernavaca.

Working in Mexico

Immigration authorities went to several small businesses and asked the managers for paperwork on several employees. After a brief investigation, it was discovered that nine people were working without proper immigration papers. While this is a story that is heard often in the United States, it actually occurred in the Lake Chapala area, just one hour from Guadalajara. (The undocumented employees were permitted to leave the country and reenter Mexico on a tourist visa.)

This story illustrates a problem for retirees in Mexico. Without the *Inmigrado* status, which provides authorization to work, a non-Mexican citizen cannot work for pay in the country.

Retirees may work in Mexico as long as their source of income is outside the nation. For example, a person who writes for a U.S. newspaper or British magazine can continue to work because the source of revenue is not Mexican.

Volunteer work is permitted, and there are numerous opportunities to spread your goodwill.

Personal Belongings

Should I bring my belongings to Mexico? The best advice is not to make this decision until you have fully checked out Mexico and made a few other decisions.

First, are you planning to live full- or part-time in Mexico? Snowbirds will probably want to keep their home in the United States completely furnished, or at least maintain a small apartment that can be used when they return north. Moving your belongings twice a year from the north to the south, and vice versa, can be expensive and troublesome.

Second, what do you really need in order to live? Some conveniences from the United States may be purchased in Mexico, but they can be expensive. For example, microwave ovens are priced at a premium in Mexico, but in the United States the same units can be purchased for less than $100. As time passes and you discover that you cannot live without that certain U.S. appliance, you may bring it down on a subsequent trip or have a visiting friend deliver it during a trip.

Finally, which visa do you hold? Depending on your status, as outlined in this chapter, there are limits to what you may bring into the country. For example, with an FM-2 visa, a retiree can bring into Mexico, tax free, household goods to furnish an average home, up to fifty books, and other articles. People on tourist visas cannot bring in items other than for immediate personal use.

It has taken you years to acquire the home furnishings and appliances that make your life more comfortable in the United States. Living-room furniture, a washer and dryer, a microwave oven, and a pasta maker—all are available on both sides of the border. Your home appliances will work in Mexico, because the same electrical current is used.

While you may be attached to many of your belongings, you will discover that Mexico is full of great things for your home. Original paintings, finely crafted wood furniture, and other home furnishings are bountiful. In fact, all the shopping that you will do in the markets will likely fill your new home quickly.

The type of clothing needed to live comfortably in Mexico depends on the city in which you settle. To help you plan, each city profile in this book includes a quick summary of the weather. In general, Cuernavaca, San Miguel de Allende, Guadalajara, and Chapala—all at higher altitudes—generally have evening temperatures in the 50s, so sweaters or jackets will be necessary.

One special item to be brought from the United States is an electric blanket, which is not available in Mexico. Retirees say that electric blankets keep away the nighttime chill in the winter months, particularly in the higher-elevation cities.

Your Health

Staying healthy in Mexico is easier than imagined. Many visitors fear Montezuma's revenge, known as *turista,* and other stomach problems. Millions of tourists visit Mexico each year, and some people do experience stomach discomforts that resolve themselves without medical attention. Retirees do not have to fall victim to this common stomach disease as long as they take precautions.

A key to avoiding problems is through prevention. "Several studies have demonstrated the effectiveness of antibiotics taken prophylactically before the illness occurs as a means of preventing traveler's diarrhea," says Agustín Escalante, a

Mexican doctor who now practices in Los Angeles. "Although tetracyclines and sulfa drugs have shown their effectiveness in prevention, they nonetheless require a prescription for their purchase."

Bismuth subsalicylate, commonly known as Pepto-Bismol, has shown some effect in preventing stomach problems when taken before traveling. U.S. doctors can offer advice before travel, particularly on what to take once in Mexico if a problem arises.

Another hint is to watch what you eat in Mexico. Food sold on the street corners may smell delicious, and the Mexicans may be lining up for it, but it is not advised for foreign travelers. Another helpful point: avoid ice, since freezing the water does not kill bacteria. When ordering a drink, simply say: *Sin hielo, por favor* ("Without ice, please").

In the new tourist areas like Cancún, new water treatment facilities have helped to make the water of drinking quality. In most cities, such as Guadalajara, Chapala, and Cuernavaca, you should only drink water that has been boiled, since common filters—even those in your home—do not remove the bacteria that cause stomach problems. This is not as inconvenient as it sounds because large quantities of boiled water can be stored in containers until needed for drinking, cooking, or brushing teeth.

Mexican Doctors

There may come an occasion to use Mexican medical services. Doctors in Mexico are like those in the United States—there are good and bad physicians. Guadalajara and Mexico City enjoy excellent medical schools that educate qualified doctors and dentists, many of whom speak some English. The U.S. government does offer assistance in this important area. For example, the U.S. Consulate in Guadalajara has a booklet called "General Information on the Guadalajara Consular District," which lists the names of area doctors.

Health Insurance

Americans living in Mexico should try to keep their U.S. health insurance policies. Medical expenses incurred in Mexico may be reimbursable by your U.S. carrier. Mexican medical insurance is also available and very affordable. For about $175 a year, retirees can sign up for the Mexican health-care system that provides complete services. There are limitations, however. As in the United States, certain preexisting conditions may not be covered by the Mexican insurance.

There is another hitch, says one retiree. When he had a heart attack, the Mexican health-care system took care of him without any questions. Two years later, he suffered a second heart attack. While the hospital treated him, he had to pay the bill because the insurance company said his heart condition was considered a preexisting one.

Money and Banking

Mexico is affordable because the country devaluates its currency almost daily, making the dollar worth more pesos every day. By checking the exchange rates in the newspapers, you can see how the strength of the U.S. dollar continues to make living in Mexico a bargain.

Retirees and experts are unanimous on one issue: pensions, Social Security, and other investments should be directly deposited into a U.S. bank. "Keep your money in the United States and keep your orientation on the dollar," says Leonard Friedman of the American-Canadian Club in Guadalajara.

Mexican banks permit accounts in pesos only. Depositing a U.S. check in a Mexican bank will translate your "cash" into *dinero*. Even though the Mexican banks pay a hefty interest rate, the interest earned is not enough to overcome the erosion of inflation or the daily peso devaluation. Your best source of security is to keep your savings in the United States.

You still should open a Mexican account, however. You will have daily expenses in Mexico: rent, food, entertainment, and household costs. Keep enough money in the Mexican bank to cover about six weeks of living expenses, which is about $1,000 for an average couple. By maintaining a six-week supply of cash in a Mexican bank, everyday living expenses can be covered without jeopardizing savings and investments in the United States.

Avoid "wiring" money from a U.S. bank to Mexico. Even if the bank is the largest in the United States, the process takes time and costs money. Instead, open an account at a Mexican bank or financial institution, such as Lloyds Associates, that will accept personal checks drawn on a U.S. bank account. This will allow you to replenish your Mexican bank account from your main U.S. bank account.

Taxes

You may not be living in the United States full time, but the U.S. government still wants its share of your income. U.S. retirees living in Mexico or elsewhere are still obligated to pay U.S. taxes. It is advisable to check with a good accountant to see how your U.S. finances should be structured to limit your tax exposure while you live in Mexico. In Mexico, however, you will not have to pay income taxes unless you have a source of revenue that is earned within the country.

Senior-citizen Discounts

Mexico knows how to take care of one of its best natural resources: its senior citizens. Mexicans in general treat people who are of *mayor edad* (older age) with great respect: the government also helps them with financial discounts. People age 60 years and older in Mexico (including U.S., Canadian, British, and other retirees) are eligible to obtain a government *INSEN* card that permits discounts of up to 30 percent on travel and other activities. People age 65 and older may receive even better discounts on international travel from Mexico.

The *Desarrollo Integral de la Familia* (DIF), which is a government agency, issues the INSEN cards. DIF offices are located in all the major cities that attract retirees, including Guadalajara, Acapulco, and Cuernavaca. To obtain the card, applicants will need to fill out a short form, provide three photos one inch in size and proof of age, such as a passport.

There are some limitations to the card, such as restricted use during the major travel seasons of Christmas and *Semana Santa* (Easter week). Nevertheless, the INSEN card is extremely useful and makes Mexico a better travel and living bargain.

Getting Your Feet Wet

▼▼▼▼▼▼▼▼▼▼▼▼▼▼▼▼▼▼▼▼▼▼▼▼▼▼▼▼▼▼▼▼▼▼▼

The best thing to do is visit Mexico. An exploratory trip will answer many of the questions you may have about living there, and it will offer you a chance to verify all the things you have heard about the nation and the people.

Homework on Mexico pays off—especially in terms of saving money and avoiding frustration. Identify the cities you would like to see, draw up an itinerary that includes visits to local retiree organizations, and make it a point to talk with people currently living in these towns. This will ensure that you have a complete picture of Mexico and all it has to offer.

3

Enjoying
Mexico

▲▲
▽▽

Retirees in Mexico mix the pleasures they enjoy in the United States, such as golf and tennis, with some uniquely Mexican activities, such as fiestas, bullfights, and concerts. Probably one of the toughest tasks a retiree will have is of deciding on which activity to select for a given day. With a little initiative and a handful of pesos, the pleasures of Mexico await retirees.

As a haven for tourists, Mexico is among the most popular countries. During the next five years, the number of tourists is expected to double to ten million annually. One reason for Mexico's increasing popularity among visitors is its range of climates.

Certainly Mexico's fantastic beaches and sunny skies usually are the images that people have of the country. In actuality, Mexico is divided into three vertical climate zones.

Tierra caliente, or the "hot land," ranges from sea level to 3,000 feet. Cancún, Acapulco, Puerto Vallarta, and other resort cities are within this lower zone. *Tierra templada,* or the "moderate land," ranges from 3,000 to 6,000 feet. Guadalajara, Cuernavaca, and other popular retirement communities are located within this range. *Tierra fría,* the "cold land," is at higher elevations that would include Mexico City, at an elevation of 7,300 feet.

The country's varied climate has spawned a multitude of activities, some related to the weather and others that have developed out of tradition or American influence. Although Mexico offers more to do than is briefly outlined in this chapter, the summaries included should provide you with a general sense of activities in the country.

Golfing

▼▼▼

Golfing may not be as popular in Mexico as it is in the United States, but there is a variety of golf courses that will tempt you to put on your spikes. From the finest 18-hole course at the Pacific resort hotel of Las Hadas in Manzanillo to the oldest greens at the Guadalajara Country Club, you will find a wide range of courses to suit amateurs and neo-pros alike.

Indeed, every city that draws a sizable number of foreign retirees has at least one course. Guadalajara, with a stable climate that makes almost every day perfect for golfing, has several good courses that will entertain and challenge golfers. (Chapters that review individual cities contain a brief listing of courses in the *Información Práctica* sections.)

Courses have their individual rules about membership and guest privileges. Retirees may be able to use the facilities of some Mexican country clubs if they present their creden-

28

tials from a U.S. country club. Private clubs often permit access only to members and their guests. Do not be discouraged, though, because these clubs sometimes allow nonmembers to use the facilities during the week.

Golf courses in resort areas, such as Manzanillo, Ixtapa, and Acapulco, are often run by hotels, but they may permit people who are not staying in the hotel to use them. While these courses may cater to tourists, they should not be overlooked by residents. For example, on the road from the airport to the resort city of Acapulco is one of Mexico's finest championship golf courses, which is shared by the Princess and the Pierre Marques hotels. Designed by Ted Robinson, this 18-hole course features a variety of water hazards. Golfing enthusiasts are encouraged to try this challenging course.

If you plan to golf regularly, it is advised that you bring your own equipment to Mexico. Golfing is considered an aristocratic sport: expect to pay accordingly for any rentals. Golf carts are often in limited supply, but caddies are readily available and eager to help.

Fishing

▼▼

Along the more than 6,000 miles of coastline, fishermen will find a place to drop their lines. Mexico has gained a reputation for marlin in the Pacific, but its waters contain an enormous variety of fish that both amateur and experienced anglers seek. Government permits, seasons, and limits are relatively liberal in favor of the fisherman.

Saltwater fishing is popular in all the resort areas, particularly in Mazatlán. Hotels often have travel desks that run daily charters, and a drive down main streets will likely bring a visitor to a charter operation. For competitive anglers, there are several popular deep-sea tournaments in Mexico. Acapulco, Cabo San Lucas, Cozumel, and other popular coastal cities host their own annual events that draw people from all over.

You do not need to go to the coast to enjoy a little angling. Freshwater fishing can keep your line in Mexico's lakes and streams. For example, fishing enthusiasts say that eight-pound bass can be fetched from the Díaz Ordaz Dam near Los Mochis, Sinaloa. Meanwhile, rainbow trout populate the rivers near Valle de Bravo in the state of México. Lake Chapala, whose banks are home to thousands of retirees, contains whitefish that are served in restaurants throughout the area.

Spas

▼▼▼

After a long day of work or recreational activities, the thought of sinking into a hot bubble bath sounds like an ideal way to loosen sore muscles. In Mexico, you can go one better by sinking into one of the many natural spas.

Warm water, naturally heated below the earth's surface, is pushed up into pools. The Indians learned of the soothing benefits of these natural pools, and the Aztec leader Moctezuma was known to frequent the outdoor spas near Mexico City. The Mexicans have harnessed the waters into recreational facilities that cater to young and old visitors alike. These spas, called *balnearios,* typically offer soothingly warm waters, natural mud packs, and massages.

Mexico's spas offer more than just hot baths, they offer relaxation. For example, the Villa Vegetariana is a health and fitness school in Cuernavaca, Morelos, that tailors programs to include low-cholesterol diets with thermal spas and walks in the countryside. This spa also relaxes your body as it enriches your mind. Classes in Spanish are offered at the spa, so retirees can keep up with their lessons.

Besides Cuernavaca, other popular retirement areas are close to these natural wonders. There are three spas near San Miguel de Allende, and the Primavera National Forest, 12 miles from Guadalajara, also features natural spas. Many of Mexico's spas can be found in the states of México, Jalisco, Querétaro, Guanajuato, Michoacán, Morelos and, of course, Aguascalientes (which means "hot waters").

Mexican Activities

Some uniquely Mexican activities, especially the bullfights and the *charreadas,* originated in Guadalajara. The pleasures of these activities can be enjoyed throughout the nation, particularly during national holidays. They provide a rich, pleasurable source of entertainment in Mexico.

Bullfighting

Of all Mexican activities, it is the bullfight that excites and intrigues visitors. Bullfights are actually called *corridas,* or "runnings," and are held in a *plaza de toros* (bullring). As almost every city in the United States has a football stadium of some size, nearly every Mexican town has a *plaza de toros.* Tickets are sold for seats in two different sections—*sol,* which is in the "sun," and *sombra,* which is in the "shade."

It has been said that bullfighting is not a sport, but an art or a "spectacle" that pits man against beast. Bullfighting follows a strict, formal routine, however, and the drama between the matador and the bull is steeped in strong Spanish tradition. Bulls are not trained; rather, they are bred to be fierce and challenging. Ranchers keep careful records of each bull's lineage because all matadors are eager to get a "good" bull that is tough, tempting and can withstand the rigors of the fight.

Bullfights may not be for every visitor, however. *Corridas* are bloody and it often appears that the bull does not have a chance of surviving the odds. Although many non-natives may want to venture into the stands to catch a glimpse of the fight, it is advised that they take seats near the exit. Since Mexicans take offense at people leaving during the event, a back-row seat can facilitate a speedy and discreet departure if the bullfight is not what you expected.

Nonetheless, *corridas* can be exciting experiences. The emotions of the crowd can easily bring you into the action, and you will walk away with a sense of having seen a Mexican tradition.

Charreadas

While bullfighting often steals the attention of visitors, it is the *charreada* (rodeo) that shows off the Mexicans' skills in training and riding animals. *Charreadas* are exhibitions of co-ordinated horsemanship, riding stunts, and roping skills. There are *charro* teams in each city, and the participants are extremely competitive and typically provide visitors with an excellent performance that should not be missed.

Called *charros* (rodeo riders), the men and women are finely dressed in elegant, handmade clothing and cowboy boots. It is here that men typically wear the large, ornately decorated *sombrero* that has become synonymous with Mexico.

Soccer

Soccer is a Mexican passion. When Mexico hosted the 1986 World Cup series, its citizens were beside themselves. One of the world's leading soccer players is a Mexican, Hugo Sánchez, and he is covered closely by the national media. Soccer, called *fútbol,* is the top sport in Mexico. The capital's stadium, Azteca, can accommodate 100,000 spectators. Guadalajara, Monterrey, and other major cities also have stadiums.

Traveling in Mexico
▼▼▼

Trains

A slight lurch forward tells you that the passenger train is gently easing out of the station. The sounds of the locomotive's engine and the rattle of the steel wheels are muffled through the nicely carpeted floor and plain, but pleasant walls. *El Constitucionalista* is about to make another one of its daily and popular runs from Mexico City to the charming colonial town of San Miguel de Allende.

Train travel in Mexico is an experience that should be enjoyed by retirees. *Ferrocarriles Nacionales de México* (National Railways of Mexico) recently renovated fourteen train routes in what is called *Servicio Estrella*, or in English, Blue Star railroad lines that run through the nation. The trains along these lines are as smooth and reliable as those found in Europe. Newspaper travel sections have helped to popularize the route through Copper Canyon, which starts from the

33

U.S.–Mexico border and continues through some of the most spectacular natural and engineering wonders of the country.

Mexico's trains crisscross much of the nation, from Guadalajara to the wonderful Pacific coast community of Manzanillo to the exciting city of Oaxaca. Railroad service is an ideal way to travel; it is convenient, extremely inexpensive, and worth the experience.

Tickets are purchased at the train station, and the popular lines (particularly during the holidays) sell out quickly. The seating on the Blue Star lines is all first class, with seats that are larger and much more comfortable than those found in airplanes. There are four classes of travel on the Blue Star lines: *primera regular* (coach), *primera especial* (special class), *camarín* (sleeper), and *alcoba* (double sleeper). Depending on the route, not all classes are available.

There are certain drawbacks to train travel, with time the most notable. A flight from Mexico City to Guadalajara takes less than an hour. A similar voyage by train takes an entire night. Also, the trains do not go everywhere travelers may desire. Despite these disadvantages, the advantages of rail travel—the excellent price, terrific service, and ideal view of the countryside—make it an excellent form of transportation.

▲▲▲

Blue Star Rail Lines

- El Centauro del Norte: Zacatecas to Durango
- El Coahuilense: Saltillo to Piedras Negras
- El Colimense: Guadalajara to Manzanillo
- El Constitucionalista: Mexico City to San Miguel de Allende

- El Tamaulipeco: Monterrey to Matamoros
- El Regiomontano: Mexico City to Nuevo Laredo
- El Tapatío: Mexico City to Guadalajara
- El San Marqueño-Zacatecano: Mexico City to Zacatecas
- El Jarocho: Mexico City to Veracruz
- El Nuevo Chihuahua-Pacífico: Chihuahua to Los Mochis
- El Oaxaqueño: Mexico City to Oaxaca
- El Purepecha: Mexico City to Uruapán
- El Rápido de la Frontera: Chihuahua to Ciudad Juárez

Airlines

Mexicana and Aeroméxico airlines provide service within the nation, as well as to many destinations in the United States. Other carriers, such as Aeromar and Aerocaribe, have routes to specific regions of the nation. Travel agents can prepare an itinerary with air service to many of the major cities in Mexico.

It must be noted that domestic flights may have open seating; after checking in, seats are on a first-come, first-served basis. In Mexico, lines form spontaneously just prior to embarking. As in the United States, airlines permit people traveling with children or others who need a little extra time the opportunity to board the plane before other passengers. If you do not fall into either of these categories, the best advice is to stay close to the gate. In Guadalajara, Acapulco, and other airports, passengers are taken from the gate to the airplane by shuttle buses.

Buses

Bus service in Mexico is actually better than its reputation would lead travelers to believe. First-class service is available in many areas, such as from Mexico City to Cuernavaca, and the quality rivals that of Greyhound in the United States.

Buses are a popular mode of transportation in Mexico. Long lines form for service between popular cities, particularly during the holidays. Some retirees have said they enjoy traveling by bus because they see more of the country and experience the people. (Bus drivers, for example, sometimes play their favorite music, while riders chat about the topics of the day.)

Several bus lines may serve the same large cities. When making your selection, peek out the station windows at the buses themselves to see which ones look the cleanest and most modern. You may pay a few extra pesos to ride on these buses, but you will enjoy the ride much more. Next, look at the schedule that is posted above the ticket window. See if the bus stops in a number of towns on its way to your destination. If you do not want to make numerous stops, choose a bus service that is more direct.

After you have selected a bus company, it is recommended that you buy your tickets about one or two hours prior to departure. Then keep an eye on the Mexican passengers. If they start forming a line for your bus, even if the departure has not been announced, you should get in line, too. This could help to avoid confusion at boarding time. Your ticket will be taken by the driver or an assistant, but you should always keep the stub.

Automobiles

Driving in Mexico gives travelers an opportunity to set their own agenda. Throughout the popular retirement area of

Lake Chapala, many of the cars are from the United States and Canada. Retirees say that having their own car gives them the ability to travel at will.

Mexican roads are in fairly good shape, with the same variety of rural and urban roads that you would expect to see in the United States. Since Mexico does not have the winter blizzards that the United States suffers, it does not have the same type of pothole problem. The federal government has pledged a massive building and improvement program to expand its highway system to more tourist areas.

Mexico's gasoline stations are government supplied, and the prices are uniform throughout the nation. Gasoline prices are occasionally raised by the government, but the rate in early 1990 was still less than a dollar a gallon. The *Petróleos Mexicanos* (Pemex) full-service stations, which are identified by their green and white colors, sell an 81-octane regular (*nova*) and a 94-octane unleaded (*sin plomo*) gasoline, as well as diesel fuels.

All types of gasoline, which is dispensed in liters, may not be available everywhere, and service station hours may vary, so residents advise maintaining a full tank. In Spanish, "fill it up" is said *lleno* (pronounced "yea-no"). While the government has the corner on the gasoline stations, you can still buy certain lubricants from Mobil, Exxon, and other oil companies throughout Mexico.

Unlike the full-service stations in the United States that also do auto repairs, Pemex stations typically only pump gasoline and clean windshields. Auto repairs are handled by privately owned garages, and finding a good one can be hit-or-miss. Have your car completely serviced before traveling to Mexico to avoid needing repairs in your retirement community. If you do need repair work done while in Mexico, a recommendation from a friend or a local retiree organization can help to narrow the list.

Mexico's champions of the road are called the *Ángeles Verdes,* or Green Angels. Operated by the Mexican Ministry of Tourism, this fleet of more than 200 specially equipped green trucks and their crews offer road service to travelers in distress. The trucks, which cruise the major highways, have bilingual crews that provide quick repairs, gasoline, and first aid.

When entering Mexico with your car, you will need a tourist visa and an importation permit for the vehicle. To complete the import forms, which can be obtained from Mexican consulates in the United States or at the border, you will need proof of ownership, a current registration card, and a valid driver's license and license plate. Remember, if you enter with your car, you must also leave with it.

Mexican drivers have a reputation for being unpredictable, so defensive driving is the best advice for dealing with traffic. The nation uses the international driving symbols on the road signs. Two signs to keep in mind include a yellow triangle that says *No Repaso,* which means "do not pass"; and *Repaso,* which means that passing is permitted.

Insurance

U.S. automobile insurance policies are not valid in Mexico. When you enter Mexico with your personal car, you will need to purchase Mexican automobile insurance. Retirees recommend purchasing an insurance policy at the border that will enable you to get to your destination. Be sure the carrier has representatives in Mexico. In the event a claim needs to be made, you will have a local representative to handle the policy.

Mexico has standardized its insurance industry, so prices are the same. The only real difference between companies is the quality of service they provide. It is important to find a company that offers bilingual service and has offices near your home.

Mexican insurance coverage is slightly different from coverage in the United States, as in the following examples:

- Personal property in the car is not covered unless it is permanently attached to the vehicle.

- There is a collision deductible on every policy. Broken glass, for example, falls under collision, and so does the deductible.

- An entire automobile must be stolen before it is covered by Mexican insurance. Vandalism and thefts of car parts are not covered.

Car Rentals

Major U.S. car rental companies—such as Avis, Hertz, and Dollar—have offices in Mexico's airports, major hotels, and popular business areas.

Inspect any rental car thoroughly before taking it off the lot. Even though you may be renting from a well-known company, do not assume that the automobile is in good shape. Besides checking it for a full tank of gasoline, check the oil, water, and windshield-wiper fluid. Tires, including the spare, should be properly filled. Cars are usually handed over in clean condition.

Ask the company about the insurance coverage and what you are specifically liable for in the event of an accident. Most automobiles use leaded gasoline, *nova,* but check with the company if it is not clearly marked in the car.

Recreational Vehicles

Recreational vehicles are an American invention that have been accommodated by the Mexicans. As increasing numbers of snowbirds discover the country, more recreational vehicles are being seen on Mexican roads.

Mobile homes, which are an ideal way to see the country without paying hotel bills, are becoming more popular among mature travelers. RV ownership among people age 55 and older has increased by 50 percent since 1980, according to the Recreational Vehicle Industry Association. RV travel is attractive because it provides retirees with home comforts, solves the problem of finding suitable housing, and offers a chance for people to go when they want. "RV retirees tend to be much more adventuresome than their contemporaries back home," according to the preeminent book on recreational vehicles in Mexico, *The People's Guide to RV Camping in Mexico,* by Carl Franz and Steve Rogers.

RV travelers in Mexico can have many of the same accommodations, such as electrical hookups, as in the United States, while they enjoy a different country, learn a language, and meet other people. There are many campgrounds throughout Mexico, particularly near the popular retirement communities of Guadalajara, San Miguel de Allende, and Cuernavaca, as well as in the beach areas of Acapulco, Mazatlán, and Puerto Vallarta. The average campground in the United States is about $14 a day; in Mexico it is about one-half that price.

Mexico's Pleasures
▼▼▼

The richness of Mexico—its people, culture, and terrain—provides a wealth of activities. Fortunately, retirees in Mexico have an opportunity to experience an ancient land and traditions in addition to the many recreational pastimes we enjoy in the United States. With a little effort and a few pesos, Mexico's best awaits Americans.

4

Mexico and Its People

A long the streets of any major Mexican city, you will see the modern age next to ancient history. Mexico's modern buildings are often connected to its colonial structures, which are built upon the stones of its ancient Indian edifices. Mexicans are constantly reminded of their past—and they are encouraged not to forget it.

Early Mexico was not a unified nation but a conglomeration of large, independent Indian populations. Among them, the Mayans dominated the south of Mexico, including the Yucatán Peninsula and Central America; and the Aztecs controlled the central part of Mexico. While the Aztecs, Mayans, and other Indian people were enjoying their reign, the Spaniards were moving westward through the Caribbean. Cuba, the West Indies, and other Caribbean islands were being conquered and settled by Spain. Mexico was next.

41

Arrival of the Spaniards

▼▼▼▼▼▼▼▼▼▼▼▼▼▼▼▼▼▼▼▼▼▼▼▼▼▼▼▼▼▼▼▼▼▼▼▼▼

Spanish explorer Hernán Cortés set foot on Antigua, Veracruz, in 1519, and unloaded his men, supplies, and horses from the ships. After everything was unloaded, he burned the ships. (Cortés scuttled his ships because he did not want his men to thwart the mission by retreating.) He then led his troops on a three-year conquest in the name of Spain that eventually leveled the Aztec empire.

The crown continued to colonize what was called New Spain, creating large *haciendas*. The settlers expanded mining operations and began exporting the riches back to the mother country. For Spanish rulers, the conquered land provided fruits beyond their imagination. Despite the growth and prosperity, inequities between the governing Spaniards and the Indian people grew—and so did discontent.

Uprisings Against the Crown

▼▼▼▼▼▼▼▼▼▼▼▼▼▼▼▼▼▼▼▼▼▼▼▼▼▼▼▼▼▼▼▼▼▼▼▼▼

Plots against Spain were discovered in the early 1790s, but the Spanish crown was able to quell all potential uprisings. It was not until an energetic priest, named Miguel Hidalgo y Costilla, who was appalled by the treatment of the Indians, worked to topple the Spanish rule in the country. Hidalgo's plot to dislodge the Spaniards began in earnest about 1810 when he rallied supporters, encouraging them to stockpile weapons and organize themselves.

Hidalgo's plans had been discovered by Spanish authorities, and they made plans to take him into custody. It was imperative that the priest act before the Spaniards seized him. At dawn on September 16, 1810, in the town of Dolores about 150 miles from Mexico City, Father Hidalgo climbed to the top of the local church and began to ring the bell to rally supporters. "Long live Mexico! Death to the *gachupines* [Spaniards]!" Father Hidalgo shouted, in what today is called *el Grito* (the yell).

What had started in the belltower in the town of Dolores would last eleven years and cost some 600,000 lives. In exchange for an end to the bloody battles, the crown and the Mexican rebels signed a pact of three guarantees: all Mexicans are equal, Roman Catholicism is Mexico's only religion, and an independent Mexico will be ruled by a constitutional monarch from Europe.

For the next several decades, political power drifted back and forth from the Liberals to the Conservatives. General Antonio López de Santa Anna—who held the presidency eleven times from 1833 to 1855—is remembered for leading the country into war with the United States in 1845. In 1846 U.S. troops marched into Mexico and captured the capital city one year later. The United States eventually withdrew and paid $15,000,000 for California, New Mexico, and Texas.

Arrival of the French
▼▼

Europe was not finished with Mexico. Britain, France, and Spain demanded that Mexico repay its outstanding debts to them; and, to secure the money, the three European powers landed troops in Veracruz in December 1861. After hearing of Mexico's intentions of improving the national economy, thus enabling the country to pay its debts at a future date, only Britain and Spain withdrew their troops, leaving Napoleon III's army in Mexico. As Hernán Cortés's forces did centuries earlier, Napoleon's troops marched into Mexico City in 1862, this time planting the French flag and Emperor Maximilian in the capital.

Maximilian's rule from a castle in Mexico City's Chapultepec Park lasted a short time. Napoleon had been withdrawing his troops to fight in Europe, leaving Maximilian vulnerable to a Mexican attack. As he attempted to flee the country, the emperor was captured by the Mexicans and executed on June 19, 1867.

Mexico's "Abraham Lincoln," Benito Juárez, assumed the presidency in 1867 with a reform agenda. Under his leadership, Mexico created a separation of church and state and abolished its colonial status.

Changes in the Twentieth Century

▼▼▼▼▼▼▼▼▼▼▼▼▼▼▼▼▼▼▼▼▼▼▼▼▼▼▼▼▼▼▼▼▼▼▼▼▼▼▼

A subsequent election brought to power a Mexican general named Porfirio Díaz, who turned his victory into a dictatorship that lasted into the twentieth century. Under the saying of "little politics, much administration," Porfirio Díaz stamped out the political opposition and focused on developing Mexico's economic resources.

Although Porfirio Díaz invited foreign investment and expanded mining and industrial activities, he failed to resolve the social and economic inequities that persisted in the country. The Mexicans, tired of a dictatorship, launched a revolution in 1910 that would last nearly a decade and cast blood across the land. Emiliano Zapata, who lead the peasants, and Pancho Villa, who rallied troops in the north, were instru-

44

mental in toppling the dictatorship of Porfirio Díaz. Díaz was forced into exile, but the country's problems and political infighting continued for years.

Eventually a coalition of labor, business, and agriculture—called the Institutional Revolutionary Party (*PRI* in Spanish)—took form in the late 1920s, which helped to end the feuds and undertake the task of running the nation. The party has dominated federal, state, and local politics since then, but today it is being challenged by well-organized opposition parties.

Meeting the Mexican People
▼▼

Mexico and its people are a rich mixture that is the product of three distinct eras: the pre-Hispanic, the colonial, and the modern. This combination has resulted in making a culture of mestizos, that is, a mixture of European and Indian blood. Although Mexico still has Indians who speak their own languages and maintain their unique cultures, most of the country is comprised of the mestizo population.

Potential retirees commonly ask: Who are the Mexicans, and will we get along? To live in Mexico and not have Mexican friends would be a shame. It is highly recommended that retirees meet and befriend as many local people as possible. Certainly there are practical reasons for forming friendships, since these new friends can help you explore the city, identify quality repair shops, and locate points of interest. The personal reasons, however, are more rewarding.

Getting to know the Mexicans has much greater, and equally tangible, benefits for retirees. Your Mexican friends will expand your horizons by offering you a different perspective of the world. Since Mexico is their nation, they can provide the link between living in the country and fully understanding it.

On an interpersonal level, *los mexicanos* are very gregarious and friendly. Americans will be amazed to hear passersby say, *buenos días* ("good morning"), when walking down the street. Also, Mexicans will likely strike up a conversation with you in a small store. Friendships can develop quickly, but they will not become as intimate as quickly— quite unlike friendships in the United States.

For example, a new Mexican friend will not immediately solicit your reasons for living in Mexico nor invite you home for dinner. You may be asked about what you think of Mexico, and you will probably hear of other sights to see that may not be mentioned in travel books. Intimate relationships take longer to develop in Mexico, but they can and will happen.

The relationship between men and women in Mexico is more complicated than in the United States. Men will speak with women, but the conversation is typically formal and not forward. It is uncommon for a man to approach a woman on the street unless he already knows her. Women, who are treated with politeness by men, are commonly entertained in groups rather than in one-on-one situations. For example, a man would not approach a woman and simply ask her to dinner that evening. The answer would likely be *no, gracias.*

Mañana: Reality

▼▼▼▼▼▼▼▼▼▼▼▼▼▼▼▼▼▼▼▼▼▼▼▼▼▼▼▼▼▼▼▼▼▼▼▼▼▼▼

People in the United States always seem to be in a rush. In a U.S. television commercial, a long-distance telephone company says that it will connect you with your caller *nine seconds* faster than its competitors. Drive-through windows at banks and fast-food restaurants are indicative of the *gringo's* desire to save time. Americans relentlessly look at their watches, a characteristic they share with Germans and Japanese. Being on time, to the minute, is important in the United States.

Mexicans, however, have a completely different concept of time, which may be difficult for Americans to understand. Americans look at time in Mexico in a laid-back fashion, which they declare on popular tee-shirts *"Mañana,* I'm on Mexican Time."

There is an order and value to time in Mexico, but it is vital to remember that Mexicans do not feel tied to the hands of a clock. Instead, they value the content of what happens during the passing of time, not the fact that time is passing. In the United States, it is said "time is money," so getting down to business has been ingrained into our psyches.

When doing business with a Mexican, for example, it is important not to lunge immediately into the transaction. For Mexicans, it is important to talk about the quality of life— family, friends, and other "small talk." Being in a rush is considered disrespectful. Despite the differences in routines, Mexicans are very hard workers who make the most of their days.

Fortunately, for retirees, time is less important. You are out of the business world, away from the daily grind, and ready for leisure. Mexico is appropriately suited for someone who wants to forget the hands of the clock and focus on the quality of life.

The typical Mexican workday begins at 9 A.M. and stops at approximately 2 P.M. for lunch. At lunchtime, almost everything—except traffic—comes to a halt. After this two-hour break, shops and offices reopen until approximately 6 or 7 P.M. Major department stores, however, are typically open from 9 A.M. to 9 P.M.

Mexico and the United States

▼▼▼▼▼▼▼▼▼▼▼▼▼▼▼▼▼▼▼▼▼▼▼▼▼▼▼▼▼▼▼▼▼▼▼▼▼▼

"Mexico, so close to the United States, so far from God." This famous Mexican saying summarizes how Mexicans feel about living in the shadow of an economically and politically stronger neighbor.

Sharing a common border does not guarantee a common agenda, and the two governments are very dissimilar. As the United States takes an active role in world affairs, Mexico follows a simple logic that was laid down by Benito Juárez: "Respect for other people's rights is peace." Typically, Mexico remains neutral or opposes intervention into another nation's affairs. When the United States invaded Panama in December of 1989, Mexico objected loudly.

While much is made of the differences between the two governments, a certain level of harmony does exist. Both countries view relations as extremely important, and efforts have been made to smooth out their differences. Every day new issues arise along the 1,900-mile U.S.–Mexican border— immigration, investment, tourism, environment, trade, and much more—that are dealt with quickly and without much attention.

Coexisting in Harmony

Certainly friction between officials from each nation occurs periodically, and this is often played out like a baseball game in the press. Nonetheless, Mexicans distinguish between U.S.

48

politics and the people from the United States. Your opinions on a variety of issues may be solicited, but Mexicans will not hold you personally responsible for actions taken in Washington, D.C. "They may not like your politics, but they will like you," says one Guadalajara resident.

Americans can coexist well with Mexicans. Daily, the bonds between the resident foreign community and the Mexican community continue to grow stronger. The Americans, Canadians, British, and other foreigners living in Mexico contribute to the economy, charities, and social climate of a very friendly nation. While Mexico may be an economically developing country, it is a very advanced society and its people know how to treat guests.

Bruce Allen, a nine-year resident of Ajijic, offers this simple suggestion to would-be residents: "If you treat Mexicans like first-class citizens, they will reciprocate in kind." An officer of a retirement organization in Guadalajara offers this advice to Americans moving to Mexico: "You're a guest in a host country. Don't tell them how to run their country; they'll make changes their way."

Mexicans have come to learn a great deal about their neighbor to the north. Because the United States plays a major role in world affairs and shares a border with Mexico, U.S. activities are constantly reported in the Mexican media. The standardized national textbook for school children deals extensively with the United States and its relations with Mexico.

Americans, from their outward appearance to their mannerisms, are a source of interest to the Mexican people. Movies, television programs, and books from the United States are available in Mexico, and the Mexicans are curious about the people from this land. Retirees may be called *gringos,* but it is not meant with disrespect.

Economics

▼▼▼

Like many countries after World War II, Mexico followed a steady pace of economic development. The economic pie was expanding in the nation's capital and in other major cities, such as Monterrey and Guadalajara. Rural economic activity took a much slower pace, and the *campesinos,* or peasant farmers, continued to stay at the lower rungs of the monetary ladder.

Then in the mid-1970s Mexico hit the jackpot—oil. Vast oil fields, which some geologists claim to be larger than Saudi Arabia's reserves, were discovered beneath Mexico's terrain. Pumping the black gold revenues into the state-owned oil company ensured political leaders that they could deliver on promises of a better tomorrow. Using the oil as a source of revenue and collateral, Mexico borrowed heavily from eager U.S. banks and other world lenders in the hope of spurring greater economic development. Billions of dollars flowed into Mexico, and the oil and natural gas seeped out of the country.

The money went for building new tourist areas, such as Cancún, and for enhancing the country's social services. Mexico's economy boomed, and soon its citizens were moving rapidly into the middle class, where they were enjoying the fruits of their new-found wealth, such as vacations in Europe and the United States.

Then the dream ended in 1982, and the economic nightmare began. The price of oil plummeted, and the Mexican government found that it could not pay the foreign banks for millions of dollars in loans. While economic problems continue today, Mexico is working to restructure its economy by pulling the government out of many industries and encouraging private foreign investment.

Government Stability

▼▼

An economic crisis is the easiest way to end a political party's dominance in government. It has happened in the United States in this century: Herbert Hoover lost to Franklin D. Roosevelt because of the Depression; Jimmy Carter lost to Ronald Reagan because of the recession. This has not been the case in Mexico, however.

Since the end of the Mexican Revolution, one party has dominated the presidency and most of the governorships. The Institutional Revolutionary Party (PRI) has controlled politics, all the state governors' offices, and a majority of the seats in the legislatures. This provided a degree of continuity for Mexico, and a majority of the people began to accept the situation. Unlike other countries, Mexico did not experience the widespread political repression that leads to popular uprisings.

The PRI is losing some of its elective seats, but the transition is taking place at the ballot box. In the 1986 and 1988 elections, the opposition gained key mayoral posts and a growing number of state legislative seats in the north. PRI presidential candidate Carlos Salinas de Gortari won his six-year term in 1986 with only a slight majority of the votes nationally, and he clearly lost to the opposition in parts of the country. This was unheard of in previous elections, as PRI candidates typically won by a landslide.

While there are doomsday preachers who say Mexico is in trouble, the evidence does not point in this direction. Mexico's opposition parties are becoming more active, which observers believe is for the best, and they are expected to continue making gains at all levels of government. The likelihood of political upheaval that has been witnessed in other developing countries is a remote possibility in Mexico.

51

5

Your Mexican Home

▲▲
▼▼▼▼▼▼▼▼▼▼▼▼▼▼▼▼▼▼▼▼▼▼▼▼▼▼▼▼▼▼▼▼▼▼▼▼▼▼

For Americans, home ownership is a way of life. Saving up a down payment, arranging financing, and then actually moving into a house is the standard procedure. In Mexico, however, acquiring a home is a different proposition.

You must make some practical decisions before you find a home in Mexico. Are you in the market for a spacious, four-bedroom house, complete with a garden or a swimming pool? Such mini-*haciendas* can be found in most cities that are popular with retirees, but they carry a premium price. You may decide to look for a two-bedroom apartment that may be more reasonably priced.

Next you must decide if owning a piece of property is really worth the time and trouble. Unlike tax laws in the United States, there are no tax breaks in Mexico for owning property.

Home mortgages cannot be found in Mexico; homes are commonly purchased outright.

It may be financially better to rent a home in Mexico rather than purchase a piece of property. Monthly rents in interior cities range from $250 to $500 a month, whereas purchasing a home may cost from $50,000 to $100,000. Without the tax advantages and given the abundance of rental properties, home ownership may not be the best option.

If home ownership is what you want, it is advisable not to purchase a home on your first visit to Mexico. Instead, residents usually recommend renting an apartment or house until you are settled into the country and its customs. After exploring the city and deciding if you really want to make such an investment, you should then try house hunting.

Finding a Rental

▼▼

For rent, downtown upstairs apartment Quinta Loreto area. 2 bedrooms, 2 baths, small garage, 2 TVs with cablevision, long-term (lease) preferred.
(From *Atención San Miguel,* San Miguel de Allende, Guanajuato.)

Ajijic two-bedroom duplex, 1-1/2 bathrooms, kitchen, completely furnished, screened porch. $300 a month.
(From *The Colony Reporter,* Guadalajara, Jalisco.)

Appealing rental housing in Mexico can be found, often at a great price. "The prices fluctuate and depend greatly on location," says one resident in Ajijic, "but bargains can be found if you put in the footwork."

Once you have decided on which city to live in and how much to spend on a place, you should prepare a plan of action to find a home. Start by taking up temporary residence in an inexpensive, conveniently located hotel that can serve as your base for house hunting. You can generally locate prospective homes with the aid of a city map, but it is much easier to rent a taxi for your hunting forays. This permits you, the house hunter, to focus on your task, rather than on navigating the city.

English-language newspapers should be the first avenue for housing leads. Classified ads in publications such as Mexico City's *The News,* Guadalajara's *The Colony Reporter,* and San Miguel de Allende's *Atención* are good leads for people seeking apartments or houses. Subscribing to them before you travel to Mexico is an ideal way to feel out the housing situation. It is important to note that the advertisements in these publications are directly geared toward foreign residents and travelers; therefore, the prices may be more expensive, though they may be reduced during negotiations with the owner.

If you are comfortable with the language, local newspapers are ideal leads for home shoppers. There are more notices listed under *Departamentos, Renta* than in the English-language media, and sometimes they contain great bargains—at prices set for the Mexican community.

Community bulletin boards and local retiree organizations are also great sources of housing leads. Stores and restaurants that Americans frequent often have bulletin boards that display housing notices. They should not be overlooked. Many Mexicans, particularly those living in communities with a large number of retirees, are accustomed to dealing with Americans, who have reputations as good renters and who may pay their monthly rent in U.S. dollars.

Officers of retirement organizations, however, ask that would-be residents travel to Mexico and visit their offices, instead of writing to them from the United States. Unfortunately, the organizations do not have printed materials to distribute, and their budgets are too small to cover postage for answering letters. By subscribing to newspapers or by buying information from people like Fran and Judy Furton, who run the organization Retiring in Guadalajara, the process can be started while you are still in the United States.

Friends who are currently living in Mexico are the best sources of information because they can help point out which neighborhoods should be considered and what are acceptable prices. Exploratory trips south of the border will undoubtedly lead to meeting retirees who are currently living there. Do not hesitate to solicit their opinions.

When touring a city, keep an eye open for signs with the words, *Se renta,* which indicate that a place is available for rent. Since newspaper advertisements can be expensive and the landlord must go to the newspaper office to pay for the announcement, it is easier to hang out a sign. This is a great way to find a bargain because only passersby will know of the unit.

What about Mexican real estate agents? With low profit margins, many Mexican real estate agents are usually uninterested in moving rental properties unless they carry a hefty monthly rent, on which they base their commissions. When it comes to purchasing a home, a real estate agent could be instrumental in leading would-be homeowners to suitable property.

Real estate is not standardized and a license is not required to sell property. If a real estate agent is sought, it is important to ask for the number of homes he or she has sold and if the company specializes in finding properties for Americans. Retirees are cautioned that real estate firms that specialize in selling property only to Americans may have a limited selection.

Purchasing a Home

▼▼

During a yearlong trip to Mexico, one writer had an opportunity to visit a small fishing village about one hour north of Acapulco. Every morning the fishermen in this village set out in their small, wooden boats to net the day's catch. The writer would relax along the beach and occasionally splash around in the clear blue water. This was heaven, and she wanted a part of it.

A local woman had a plot of land to sell, which seemed like a good deal. While gathering up the necessary cash to buy the home, the writer sought the advice of an attorney. After a little digging, the attorney discovered that the property was an *ejido,* which is given by the government to a family as part of land reform. It put a halt to the sale. If the writer had purchased the land, the seller could have demanded the property back at any time—without refunding the money.

While this story has a mixed ending—the land was actually unavailable—buying a home or condominium in Mexico is possible. Regulations governing foreign ownership of property have been liberalized, and that is good news for retirees who want to purchase a home.

Lawyers, called *abogados* in Spanish, are not necessary for renting a home, but they can be helpful when purchasing one. Banks or retiree organizations will recommend a reliable attorney.

Contracts aside, a retiree has to be sure that the property can actually be sold by the owner. Titles, which are proof of ownership, can have stipulations in them that can halt the sale or even require that the new owner return the property without any compensation. Title search companies will examine the deed for you; check it for any liens, errors, inaccuracies, or other problems; and issue a report. Experts say this could provide a purchaser with the necessary safeguards for dealing with property ownership in a foreign country.

The appeal of living in Mexico has fostered the development of retirement communities, or complexes, that include complete apartments, recreation areas, and security. Retirees may want to consider these developments, which can be found along the coast and in the interior, but they are likely to be more expensive than conventional Mexican homes.

A Quick List

▼▼▼▼▼▼▼▼▼▼▼▼▼▼▼▼▼▼▼▼▼▼▼▼▼▼▼▼▼▼▼▼▼▼▼▼▼

When you examine a house or an apartment, you should check the following features:

- Does the property have two gas tanks?

- How should the renter arrange to have the gas tanks replaced when they are empty?

- Because Mexico can experience water shortages, homes typically have a reserve water tank on the roof. Be sure one is in place and is fully operational.

- If you are thinking of hiring a maid, will there be live-in quarters for her? Maids who come only for the day also require a room for changing and the use of a restroom.

- As in any dwelling, plumbing and electrical fixtures may need repair. Arrange in advance to have all broken items fixed, and establish a procedure for having items fixed in the future. Landlords are expected to handle major repairs, but the renter is responsible for minor improvements, such as painting.

- Is there a telephone? If not, it could take longer than one year to have a line installed.

- Where is the nearest post office? Letter carriers in Mexico only deliver the mail. A person must go to the post office to send mail.

- Finally, food shopping in Mexico is usually done every day, with fresh fruit, produce, and meat being purchased for the day's meals. Ask the landlord where the nearest market is located and visit it to see if you would like shopping there.

Mexico has a variety of homes available at a range of prices. After getting through the practical decisions—price and location—the actual selection process can go fairly smoothly. A degree of legwork will be needed, but a good home can be found. Then you can settle into enjoying Mexico.

6

La Perla del Occidente

▲▲▲
▽▽▽▽▽▽▽▽▽▽▽▽▽▽▽▽▽▽▽▽▽▽▽▽▽▽▽▽▽▽▽▽▽▽▽▽▽

Guadalajara

▼▼▼

G uadalajara is synonymous with American retirement in Mexico. When a chill begins to set in across the northern part of the continent, a steady stream of American and Canadian snowbirds join the more than 40,000 resident seniors in this Mexican refuge from the cold.

Retirees are drawn to Guadalajara for many reasons other than climate. The city is a unique, comfortable blend of classic Spanish and indigenous cultures, all topped off by modern Mexico. To live in Guadalajara is to feel and be a part of a thriving culture.

Spanish *conquistadores* reached the area in 1541, some 20 years after the fall of the Aztecs in Mexico City. They turned Guadalajara into an outpost in New Spain's central plateau. Drawing on the traditions of their homeland, the Spanish settlers erected grand government buildings out of hand-cut, hand-placed stones and designed charming plazas to complement their structures. The resulting colonial architecture and town planning have earned Guadalajara the title of *La perla del occidente* ("The Pearl of the West").

Downtown Guadalajara is a living testament to Spanish design. Central to the area is the popular cathedral—a twin-towered structure that was started in 1558 and completed six decades later. Interestingly, the cathedral's architectural style has been described as "dizzying" because it is a combination of Gothic, Byzantine, Tuscan, Corinthian, Doric, and Baroque. The generations spent building this colossal stone and mortar structure and the ensuing architectural tastes, as well as an earthquake in 1848 that destroyed the original towers, resulted in this unique blend. The nearly 400-year-old cathedral is rich in other history: Spanish explorers, colonizers, and religious leaders knelt before the altar and asked for God's blessings.

Five Fabulous Plazas

Traditionally, Spanish designers would accent a large building, like the cathedral, with a town square. Not content with one charming plaza, the Spaniards decided to build four wonderful plazas around the cathedral. The four one-block plazas—*Laureles, Rotonda de los Hombres Ilustres, de los Tres Poderes* (formerly *Liberación*), and *de Armas*—surround the cathedral with fountains, trees, and monuments.

In 1982, the city completed an eighteen-acre plaza, *Tapatío,* that unites many of the colonial buildings near the cathedral. The park is a living tribute to the people of Guadalajara, who call themselves *tapatíos*. Besides the traditional fountains, trees, and shrubbery, the plaza features handwrought iron lamps and a 68-foot bronze sculpture marking the arrival of the first Spanish settlers. A long mural, praising the development of Mexico and encouraging its citizens to remain independent, occupies an enormous section of a wall facing the *Plaza Tapatío*.

The network of five plazas and surrounding commerce forms the center of activity in Guadalajara. On any warm Sunday, directly in front of the historic cathedral, the plaza bustles with more than one hundred people of all ages— enjoying frozen yogurt, drinking sodas, and relaxing in the afternoon sun. Street musicians pour out melodies for listeners; nearby, young men peddling goods chime in with their own special blend of music.

Cabañas Cultural Institute

The Guadalajara experience does not end with the plazas. One of the largest colonial buildings ever constructed in the Americas is situated at the eastern end of the *Plaza Tapatío*. Covering six acres that feature twenty-three patios and a large reflecting pool, the Cabañas Cultural Institute is as impressive as the plazas themselves. It was originally built in 1810 as a refuge for the poor and orphans of the state of Jalisco. The buildings and grounds are now open to the public.

Mexico's famous muralist José Clemente Orozco put his mind and paintbrush to work on the institute's walls and ceilings in 1938 and 1939. Clemente's brilliant work depicts scenes from Mexico's struggle for independence from colonial rule and the revolution that occurred more than one hundred years later. The master's work—with its vibrant colors, sweeping pictorials, and larger-than-life characters—will keep visitors in awe. In the main building of the institute, Clemente painted images on the ceiling. The institute provides mirrors so visitors can see the artwork without straining their necks.

The institute does not limit its displays to Clemente's work. The artwork of other artists, particularly of students from the local university, is also displayed, which helps to bring visitors back to the Cabañas Cultural Institute. Some of the pieces are for sale, and a small bookstore sells books on various artists' works.

Like the Cabañas Cultural Institute, other buildings near the cathedral and the plazas are exciting to visit. The *Palacio Municipal,* the local government palace, is a building made of hand-cut stone that features a graceful and charming interior. Inside the Palacio Municipal is a striking mural called *Los Fundadores* ("The Founders"), which was painted between the main staircases by the artist Gabriel Flores.

It is easy to get around old downtown Guadalajara, which makes taking in the sights simple and enjoyable. Indeed, it is best seen on foot, with plenty of opportunities to rest. Despite its popularity and its somewhat chaotic urban surroundings, old Guadalajara remains in excellent shape and has earned a grand reputation.

Beyond Colonial Downtown

Guadalajara is ideal for golfing, tennis, walking, and other outdoor activities. With a stable climate and a four-month rainy season that usually brings precipitation in the early evening, the daylight hours are ideal for being outside. Retirees note that it takes a little while to get accustomed to the 5,000-foot altitude, so at first they take it easy on the golf course.

In addition to golfing, retirees in Guadalajara may choose from a variety of activities. Popular U.S. films shown in local movie houses, English-language theater, and social events fill up people's calendars. One American spent so much time attending social functions and going sightseeing that he forgot to go house hunting. He eventually had to adjust his schedule to accommodate life's daily chores.

Many romantic images of Mexico—*mariachis,* tequila, *charros,* and the classic *vaqueros* (cowboys)—have drawn retirees and tourists to Guadalajara. This rich flavor of Guadalajara is enjoyed by retirees, particularly when friends from back home come down for a visit. For example, *mariachis,* small groups of musicians and singers who perform in parks and liven up Mexican parties, are a pleasure to listen to and watch.

Mexicans love *fiestas,* and residents in the state of Jalisco do their part to satisfy their demands. The state sponsors the annual *Fiestas de Octubre en Guadalajara,* the Mexican version of Octoberfest, a month of art and culture. Visitors can see fantastic artwork, folkloric dances, and local talent throughout the month.

Shopping in Guadalajara

From handmade crafts to locally distilled tequila, Guadalajara is a shopper's paradise. For people visiting Guadalajara's bustling downtown area, there are many interesting shops that are easily accessible on foot. The *Plaza de las Sombrillas* (parasols) is an open-air pedestrian zone that features both large stores and small shops. It is situated just west of the *Plaza de los Laureles.*

The *Mercado Libertad* offers a uniquely Mexican shopping experience. Under the market's enormous roof, fruits, vegetables, and household items are sold in stands. The market is located near *Plaza Tapatía* on Avenida Javier Mina. You should not miss the chance to experience this unique, but typically Mexican, market.

Guadalajara

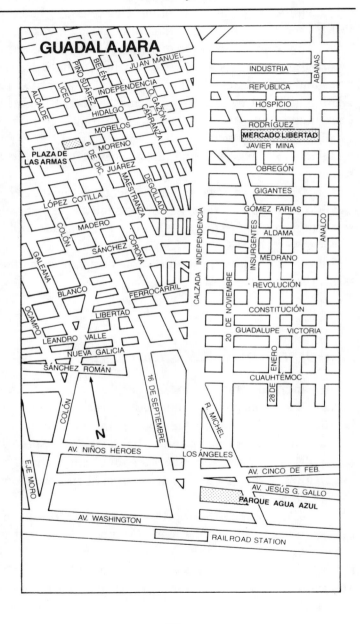

To get away from traditional shopping, Guadalajara features a working glass factory. The *Fábrica de Vidrio Soplado*, located at Medrano 281, is a unique glass factory in which visitors are invited to watch glass being blown into shape. Visitors can purchase inexpensive products there.

Serious shoppers should not overlook two of Guadalajara's best-known shopping areas. *Tlaquepaque* and *Tonalá*, two of Guadalajara's suburban towns, feature some of the finest handmade crafts in the region. You could spend an entire day shopping in this arts-and-crafts paradise.

▲▲▲▲▲▲▲▲▲▲▲▲▲▲▲▲▲▲▲▲▲▲▲▲▲▲▲▲▲▲▲▲▲▲▲▲▲▲

Información Práctica

Population: 4,000,000
Altitude: 5,209 feet
Weather: If temperature and climate are why you want to be in Mexico, then Guadalajara is a top choice. The four-month rainy season begins in June, with an average rainfall of 7.6 inches; continues through July (10 inches) and August (7.9 inches); and ends in September (7 inches). It typically rains in the early evening or at night, leaving the morning air clean and fresh. The remaining months average less than an inch of rain.

The temperature is stable throughout the year. In December the average temperature is about 65 degrees, while May tips the thermometer at 76 degrees. Residents say the nights are cool, typically in the 50s.

Housing: As more retirees and Mexicans choose to make Guadalajara their home, the price of housing is climbing, but it is still relatively affordable. Resident experts peg the prices of rental apartments from $200 to $400 a month; homes are approximately $400 to $600 a month. The English-language weekly newspaper *The Colony Reporter* lists some rentals and sales.

Museums: Centro de Arte Moderno, Mariano Otero 375, is one of the finest galleries for a variety of artwork; *Instituto de la Artesanía Jalisciense,* Avenida Independencia in Parque Agua Azul, features handicrafts such as pottery, ceramics, saddlery, and furniture; *Museo Arqueológico del Occidente,* at Avenida Independencia and Plaza Juárez, features Indian artifacts from Jalisco, Colima, and Nayarit; *Museo Orozco,* Calle Aurelio Aceves 27, features a variety of the artist's work including a room devoted exclusively to his sketches of the 1910 Revolution. There are numerous other galleries and museums that should be visited.

Music: Mariachis are a Guadalajaran export. One of the best places to see them swarming like bees is at the *Plaza de los Mariachis,* where the musicians wait to be hired for a single song, an hour, or an entire evening. While you can see a handful of them performing in the plaza during the day, the nighttime is best for enjoying their music and observing their salesmanship. There are many outdoor cafés for people to sit and witness the goings-on. The plaza is located next to the Mercado Libertad at Avenidas Javier Mina and Independencia.

Rodeos: Guadalajara invented the *charreada,* or Mexican rodeo. Near the railroad station and Parque Agua Azul is the *Aceves Galindo Lienzo,* where each Sunday horsemen and cowboys put on wonderful performances.

Golfing: Club de Golf Santa Anita, 18 holes, is open to the public on weekdays (telephone: 21-61-86). *Guadalajara Country Club,* located at Mar Caribe 260, has an 18-hole, 72-par golf course open only to members and their guests (telephone: 41-19-65). *San Isidro Golf Club* is an 18-hole course that is located at Bosques San Isidro Norte. It is open to the public on weekdays (telephone: 33-15-06). *Club de Golf Atlas,* Km 6 of Carretera Guadalajara-Chapala, is an 18-hole course that is open to visitors on weekdays (telephone: 35-82-98). *Club de Golf Rancho Contento* can be reached by calling 21-68-89.

Tennis: Guadalajara Racquet Club is an exclusive, expensive location for tennis and squash. Several hotels have tennis courts, including the *Camino Real, El Tapatío,* the *Fiesta Americana,* and the *Holiday Inn.*

Transportation: Airport: The Aeropuerto Internacional Miguel Hidalgo is located about 8 miles from the city, which is about a twenty-minute drive. Vans can provide transportation to hotels and homes at very reasonable rates.

Bus Station: Guadalajara's newest station, *Central Camino,* is a modern facility on the outskirts of town. Buses leaving from this station provide service to Chapala and other parts of Mexico.

Trains: Trains arrive in downtown Guadalajara at the south end of Calzada Independencia. The popular, renovated Blue Star railroad line from Mexico City to Guadalajara, *El Tapatío,* arrives at this station. *El Tapatío* is an overnight ride to the nation's capital.

Spas: El Tapatío is a first-class hotel and resort that offers saunas, tennis, horseback riding, and other activities with discounts for seniors. (El Tapatío, Blvd. Aeropuerto No. 4275, Guadalajara, Jalisco; telephone: 35-60-50.) *Rancho Río Caliente,* located about 20 minutes northwest of Guadalajara in the Primavera National Forest, is a vegetarian health spa. The thermal waters can be taken in a hotel bath or in a swimming pool. (Río Caliente, Apartado Postal 1-1187, Guadalajara, Jalisco; telephone: 15-78-00; U.S. telephone: 213-796-5577.)

Hotels: There are so many hotels in Guadalajara, only a handful can be listed here:

- *Camino Real,* Avenida Vallarta 5005; telephone: 47-00-80; U.S. telephone: 800-228-3000.
- *El Tapatío Country Club and Spa,* Blvd. Aeropuerto No. 4275; telephone: 35-60-50. Senior discounts are available.
- *Plaza del Sol,* Mariano Otero y López Mateos Sur; telephone: 47-87-90; U.S. telephone: 619-585-3409.
- *Hotel Calinda Roma,* Avenida Juárez 170; telephone: 14-86-50. The hotel gives discounts to members of senior-citizen clubs.
- *Motel Isabel,* Montenegro 1572; telephone: 26-26-30. Pets are accepted.
- *Hotel de los Reyes,* Calz. Independencia y López Cotilla; telephone: 13-00-76.

RV Parks: Centro Vacacional Agua Caliente is at Km 16 in Villa Corona near Mexico Highway 80. *Guadalajara Trailer Park* is located at Highway 54 and Avenida Alcalde (mailing address: Apartado Postal 1-2062, Guadalajara, Jalisco; telephone: 23-13-17). The *Hacienda Trailer Park* is situated on Highway 15 on the west side of Guadalajara (mailing address: Apartado Postal 5-494, Guadalajara, Jalisco; telephone: 21-50-84). *PAL RV Park* is located on the southwest side of town at Avenida

Turquesa and Agua Marina (mailing address: Apartado Postal 1-1470, Guadalajara, Jalisco; telephone: 21-90-50). *Pirámide Trailer Park* is at Km 15 on the Periferico Sur, near the archeological zone (mailing address: Apartado Postal 31-307, Guadalajara, Jalisco). *San José del Tajo Trailer Park* can be reached by writing to Apartado Postal 31-242, Guadalajara, Jalisco; or by calling 86-14-95.

English-language Bookstores: Sandi Bookstore has a large assortment of new books and U.S. publications, as well as *The Mexico City News* and *The Colony Reporter.* The store is also a local gathering place for retirees (address: Tepeyac 718, Colonia Chapalita; telephone: 21-08-63). *Sanborn's* is a popular restaurant that also sells English and Spanish publications. There are two Guadalajara locations: one is next to the Hyatt Regency Hotel; the other is at Avenida Vallarta, close to Avenida Chapultepec.

Library: Ben Franklin Library has a wide selection of books, as well as back issues of selected periodicals. It is located in the same building as the U.S. Consulate (Libertad 1492; telephone: 19-04-80).

Religious Services: Baptist: Gethsemane Baptist Church, Colomos 2148 (telephone: 42-22-15). *Catholic:* Catedral de Guadalajara, Alcalde and Hidalgo. Saint Mary's Catholic Church, Tepeyac and Zumárraga, Colonia Chapalita (telephone: 21-38-22). *Episcopal:* Saint Mark's Episcopal Church, located at Aztecas and Chichimecas (telephone: 31-99-51). *Jewish:* Sinagoga, located at Yaquis 651 (telephone: 41-64-11). *Lutheran:* All Saints Lutheran Church, Avenida Tepeyac (telephone: 21-67-41). *Protestant:* Services are held at the Primera Iglesia Bautista, Independencia Sur and Medellín.

Lake Chapala and Environs
▼▼▼▼▼▼▼▼▼▼▼▼▼▼▼▼▼▼▼▼▼▼▼▼▼▼▼▼▼▼▼▼▼▼▼▼▼

Lake Chapala attracts migrating snowbirds who seek to get away from the freezing temperatures in the north. Wealthy *tapatíos* also slip away to Lake Chapala, situated only 45 minutes from Guadalajara, for a vacation or weekend retreat from the big city.

The lake is not a secret. Lake Chapala is the nation's largest inland body of water, which stretches to 60 miles in length and from 12 to 20 miles in width. Low mountains cradle the shallow lake, and the view as you drive from Guadalajara into Chapala is attractive.

The calm lake is a pleasure for water activities, and sailboats are available for rent. Guided trips around the lake are also available and are recommended by the locals. For those who prefer the fruits of the water, Lake Chapala is best known for its whitefish, which is famous throughout Mexico. Local restaurants take pride in their fresh whitefish recipes, and local retirees highly recommend sampling them. On dry land, the banks are abundant with wonderful scenery and migrating birds that winter along the lake's shores.

Chapala

The community of Chapala maintains a quaint, small-town charm. There is only one traffic light in this town of approximately 40,000 people. As you sit in a sidewalk café at the one-traffic-light intersection, you will notice that about fifty percent of the passersby are American and most of the cars on the street feature license plates from places outside Mexico—California, Texas, Utah, Wyoming, and even Ontario, Canada. The constant influx of Canadian, British, and U.S. retirees, however, has not diluted the charm of the area.

Because of the high concentration of English-speaking residents in Chapala, most of the merchants who cater to these individuals have learned to communicate well with their limited-Spanish-speaking patrons. Restaurants and shops typically have bilingual waiters and sales attendants to assist tourists and retirees. Restaurants feature English-language menus and signs in their windows that advertise homes for rent.

Chapala is a clean, well-kept community that has a friendly atmosphere. The buildings along Avenida Madero, the principal street, are in good shape and many are freshly painted. Structures along the side streets are in similarly good condition.

Avenida Madero, which originates from the shores of Lake Chapala, is the main shopping and business district. But do not expect the mall scene. Unlike Guadalajara, Chapala is a quiet community that does not offer much in the way of shopping. Pharmacies, handicraft stores, and restaurants are the typical businesses along Avenida Madero. Since Chapala is less than an hour away from Guadalajara, retirees who love to shop can easily take a day-trip to the "big city."

Retirees and other residents in Chapala are very friendly, and they have created a nice social atmosphere. There are plenty of activities, including golfing, fishing, and participation in retirement organizations. Of the local sights to see, an out-of-service 1920s train station is unique and attractive, as are the local mansions of some of the wealthy Guadalajarans who weekend along the lake.

▲▲

Información Práctica

Population: 40,000.
Altitude: 5,000 feet.

Weather: Chapala's weather is very similar to Guadalajara's weather, which makes it all the more popular with retirees. The "lake effect" helps to keep Chapala and other nearby communities slightly warmer in the winter and cooler in the summer than in the metropolis of Guadalajara. The average humidity ranges from 20.9 to 57.8 percent, a local organization reports. During the rainy season, the rain typically falls from 9 P.M. to 4 A.M.

Housing: Housing and basic living needs are slightly more expensive in Chapala than in Guadalajara, but that is to be expected because Chapala is thought of as a resort area. Purchase prices of homes range from twenty-five thousand dollars to more than several million U.S. dollars. It is estimated that an average three-bedroom home costs $80,000. Rental prices range from $400 to $600 a month.

Rental and sales notices are placed in restaurants along Avenida Madero. With the growing popularity of Chapala, real estate offices are opening in the area.

Golfing: Club Privado Cerrito Blanco is located at the outskirts of Chapala on the road from Guadalajara. The *Chapala Country Club* and the *Chula Vista Country Club* are available for use.

Transportation: Buses run hourly from Guadalajara, leaving from the new terminal and arriving in Chapala 45 minutes later. In Chapala, the terminal is located on Avenida Madero, about six blocks from the lone traffic light. There is regular two-way taxi service to the Guadalajara international airport, which is about 30 miles away.

Hotels: *Hotel Nido,* located at the traffic light on Avenida Madero 202, is a nice old hotel with a huge, open lobby. Hotel Nido also has a restaurant and bar (telephone: 765-21-16). *Hotel Villa Montecarlo,* Avenida Hidalgo 296, is situated on the lake and has a thermal pool (telephone: 765-21-20). *Hotel Chapala Hacienda,* Km 40, is a budget hotel (telephone: 765-27-20).

RV Parks: *PAL RV Park* has daily and monthly rates. It is situated between Chapala and Ajijic and features 110 sites (telephone: 762-90-50). For information, write to PAL, Apartado Postal 1-1470, Guadalajara, Jalisco.

Religious Services: *Little Chapel by the Lake,* on Blvd. Ajijic between Chapala and Ajijic, offers nondenominational services.

Ajijic

▼▼

Since D. H. Lawrence wrote *The Plumed Serpent* in Ajijic, the town has developed a reputation as a writers' community. While a few residents fancy themselves as writers and artists, Ajijic has attracted a diverse crowd of retirees and other residents.

Like its neighbors of Chapala, Chula Vista, and Jocotepec, Ajijic is part of the Gold Coast of Lake Chapala. Ajijic is an extremely quiet town that lends itself to reading, relaxing, and having small get-togethers. Local natural spas are a big attraction for tourists, but locals note that these visitors do not stay too long.

Ajijic is laid-back, but it is not boring. Unlike other cities, where entertainment may be ready-made, residents in Ajijic make their own fun. Many people enjoy shopping in the little stores that sell a variety of handmade products. In February, residents compete in an internationally sanctioned chile cook-off, with the proceeds going to local charities.

Ajijic's streets are a combination of cobblestone and dirt, with sidewalks that are narrow but adequate for pedestrian traffic. The locals relish the town's quaintness. On one Monday afternoon, many of the streets were filled with more American equestrians than motorists. The riders, laughing and talking among themselves, trotted along in groups of three or four.

Those who relocate to Ajijic seem to enjoy it. "I sold everything back home in Washington and moved down here to Ajijic. It was the best decision I've made since retiring," said a 70-year-old gentleman who now lives along Lake Chapala. He boasted of his home with a 64-foot balcony overlooking the lake, and of the fact that he has a maid who sweeps the balcony.

▲▲▲

Información Práctica

Population: 20,000.
Altitude: 5,000 feet.
Weather: Same as in Chapala.
Housing: The *Hotel Posada* has a bulletin board that features housing notices. Residents say that to find a home in Ajijic, you should contact the locals and then endure some legwork. Rental units run about $250 to $500 a month.

Transportation: From Chapala, local buses leave from Avenida Madero, about one block from the main bus terminal. The twenty-passenger vehicles run along Avenida Madero and Ajijic Boulevard. The ride lasts about twenty minutes, and the driver will let passengers off at any spot along the route. There are no formal bus stops; just wave your hand and the passing bus will stop.

Spas: Balneario San Juan Cosala, which is situated between Ajijic and Jocotepec, features seven pools.

Hotels: Hotel Posada, 16 de Septiembre and Morelos, offers nice rooms and has a pool (telephone: 765-33-95). It also has a bulletin board listing local information. *Hotel Mariana,* at Guadalupe and Marc Castillanos, offers daily, weekly, and monthly rates. *Hotel Danza del Sol,* Zaragoza 165, is in a colonial building. *Hotel la Floresta,* Paseo del Mirador 4, is a moderately priced hotel.

RV Parks: PAL RV Park (see the listing for Chapala).

Library: Library Ajijic, 16 de Septiembre 16-A, has a collection of English-language reading material. In addition, it holds meetings, sponsors a Spanish-language program for children, and provides equipment for disabled persons and talking textbooks for the blind. The library cannot answer written requests for retirement information.

7

Central Cities

San Miguel de Allende

To live in San Miguel de Allende is to live in a postcard of colonial Mexico. When arriving by train, passengers step into a small, well-kept station that looks as though it were transplanted from a toy train set. San Miguel's downtown streets are a joy for the eyes and ears. It is fun to listen to the bumpity sound of cars driving noisily over the cobblestones. Colonial structures surround the main downtown plaza, and during the afternoons, scores of people of all ages gather to read, talk, and enjoy the scenery.

San Miguel de Allende is colonial Mexico with a splash of modern art. It is quaint, picturesque, highly relaxing, and intellectually stimulating. These qualities continue to attract retirees to the city, which has managed to absorb the growing number of snowbirds and full-time residents without many problems.

Modern Retirement

Up to three thousand English-speaking retirees call San Miguel de Allende home year-round, and the snowbirds easily increase that number during the winter months. San Miguel de Allende will continue to be a popular city for full- and part-time retirement, and more houses are being built at the outskirts of town to handle the demands of retirees.

Art and writing are among the top reasons why retirees seek out San Miguel de Allende. Community schools offer a wide selection of English-language classes in drawing, painting, writing, and other subjects. San Miguel de Allende, which is relatively small, provides a diversity in these areas of study that probably rivals the offerings in many state capitals and cities of larger size.

Of all the schools, the *Instituto Allende,* started in 1938 by Stirling Dickenson, continues to be one of the finest in the state. Americans have attended the Instituto Allende since the end of World War II, when the GI Bill made it easy for former soldiers to enroll. As the school's popularity grew, the former governor of Guanajuato turned over an old hacienda, the eighteenth-century palace of the Counts of Canal, so the institute could grow. Today, the school continues to draw enrollees, and many well-known professors and professionals are guest teachers. All the classes are taught in English, but the institute does offer Spanish-language instruction.

Certainly the Instituto Allende draws much of the attention, but there are other schools in the city that have fine curricula. The *Academia Hispano Americana* is a small school that focuses on teaching Spanish, history, and literature. The school's classes, which run from one to twelve weeks, are small and intensive. Residents wanting to learn basic Spanish can look into the school *Inter Idiomas,* whose classes average about six students.

San Miguel de Allende's residents have other resources at their disposal in the nation's largest bilingual library, *La Biblioteca Pública*. Its shelves feature classic and contemporary titles, including a few written by local residents. In addition to its holdings, the library is the gathering center for many residents, and it houses the offices of the local newspaper, *Atención*.

Day-trip Destination: Guanajuato

Living in San Miguel de Allende puts residents close to the terrific city of Guanajuato, the state's namesake. The city, built in the Sierra Madre mountains on the banks of the Río Guanajuato, is a former silver-mining town that is rich in many other special ways.

Guanajuato's narrow streets are buttressed by colorful buildings that feature flower-encircled balconies. One alley is called *el Callejón del Beso* (the Street of the Kiss) because two lovers, forbidden by their parents to see each other, would rendezvous by simply leaning from their balconies for a simple kiss. In addition to stirring romance, Guanajuato's colonial streets incorporate small boutiques, sidewalk cafés, and quaint hotels.

Guanajuato's streets fill with other exciting activities. The annual *International Cerventino Festival* draws performers and spectators from around the world for two weeks of art, music, and dance. Typically held at the end of October, the International Cerventino Festival is a cultural event that is on the must-see calendar of retirees and tourists alike. It is worth the trip from San Miguel de Allende.

Thousands of Canadian and American retirees call San Miguel de Allende home. Although train and bus services are available to San Miguel de Allende, the nearest international airport is four hours away in Mexico City.

▲▲▲

Información Prtica

Population: 55,000.

Altitude: 6,134 feet.

Weather: San Miguel de Allende has a wonderful, stable temperature that ranges from 57 to 68 degrees. March and April are typically dry months. The July to September rainy season brings a monthly average of an inch or more of precipitation.

Housing: Furnished apartments begin at $150 a month. The biweekly English-language newspaper, *Atención,* lists numerous rental and sale leads. The bulletin board at Instituto Allende also features hand-posted listings, as well as some of the businesses in the downtown area.

Golfing: Club de Golf Malanquín is a 9-hole course.

Transportation: Bus station: This is a one-room building near Calle de los Órganos and Avenida Insurgentes. Buses depart to Guanajuato and elsewhere.

San Miguel de Allende

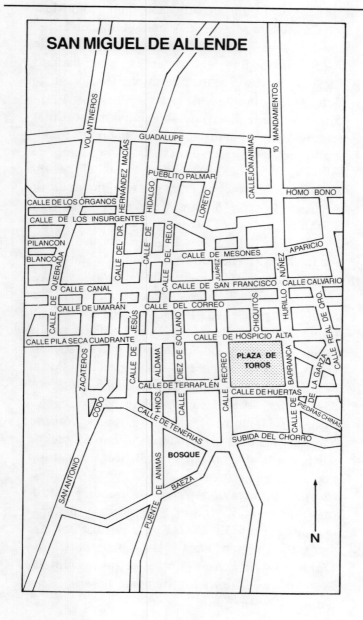

83

Trains: Excellent *Servicio Estrella Azul* (Blue Star Service) transports travelers daily from Mexico City to San Miguel de Allende. The train leaves the capital at 7 A.M. and arrives in San Miguel de Allende about four hours later. The train back to Mexico City leaves in the afternoon. Tickets can be purchased at the station.

Spas: Balneario Hacienda Taboada is a resort that features thermal baths and swimming pools (mailing address: Apartado Postal 100, San Miguel de Allende, Gto. 37700; telephone: 652-08-88). *Parador El Cortijo* is a hotel and spa (mailing address: Apartado Postal 585, San Miguel de Allende, Gto. 37700; telephone: 652-17-00).

Hotels: The *Aristos San Miguel* is located across the Instituto Allende on Calle Ancha de San Antonio (telephone: 652-01-49). The *Posada San Francisco,* a quaint 50-room hotel, is located on the *zócalo* (telephone: 652-14-66).

RV Parks: Lago Dorado KDA has 65 sites and is situated southwest of San Miguel de Allende off Highway 51 (mailing address: Apartado Postal 523, San Miguel de Allende, Gto.). *La Siesta Motel & RV Park,* located south of San Miguel de Allende off Highway 51, offers 70 spaces. *Rancho San Ramón,* which is northwest of San Miguel de Allende at Km 5 on Highway 51, features natural pools and picnic areas.

English-language Bookstores: Surrounding the *zócalo* are sidewalk vendors that sell daily newspapers and periodicals. *El Colibrí,* located at Portales and Calle Umarán, has the latest bestsellers.

Library: La Biblioteca Pública, at Insurgentes 25, is one of the nation's top bilingual libraries (telephone: 652-10-17).

Religious Services: St. Paul's Episcopal Church is located near the Instituto Allende (mailing address: Apartado Postal 268, San Miguel de Allende, Gto. 37700; telephone: 652-03-28).

Cuernavaca

▼▼

Cuernavaca continues to be a major retirement city, as well as a popular weekend retreat from crowded Mexico City. It is referred to as the city of "eternal spring" because of its natural springs and bountiful forests. For thousands of Americans and Canadians, Cuernavaca is a blend of cosmopolitan living and quiet retirement.

Cuernavaca's appeal as a retreat is ancient. The Aztec ruler Moctezuma, Hernán Cortés, and Emperor Maximilian all used Cuernavaca as their haven from the capital city. The Aztecs originally called it *Cuauhnáhuac,* which meant "at the edge of the forest," and their leaders sought its peace and solace. The Spaniards, however, found the name to be too difficult to pronounce, and they renamed it *Cuernavaca,* which means a "cow's horn."

Spanish King Charles V awarded Hernán Cortés the city of Cuernavaca as a bounty for his explorations, and the conqueror wanted to make it his Mexican retirement home. Although Cortés built a mansion there, he died in Spain in 1547 and could not live out his plan. Nonetheless, the Spaniards made good use of the region by designating huge areas for hunting grounds. Emperor Maximilian, who ruled Mexico for about five years, built his personal retreat in Cuernavaca in 1865. Maximilian reportedly found Cuernavaca's summer climate to be much more enjoyable than Mexico City's.

Like previous retirees, today's seniors find Cuernavaca to be convenient to Mexico City and its big-city offerings, but distant enough to insulate them from the rigors of the metropolis. Cuernavaca has numerous attractions to ensure that you can avoid Mexico City other than to use the international airport.

Cuernavaca is known for its beautiful homes surrounded by high walls. Former elected officials, businessmen, and the elite of Mexico City maintain sanctuaries there. While much is made of the mansions behind walls, Cuernavaca also has large parks and museums that are open to the public.

The Riches of Cuernavaca

Cuernavaca's famous landmark on the *zócalo,* the *Palace of Cortés,* is a museum that is rich in the country's history. Diego Rivera's sweeping, colorful murals cover an entire wall of the 470-year-old palace, which housed the state legislature at one time. Rivera, Mexico's political painter, had been commissioned by U.S. Ambassador Dwight Morrow to portray major events in the nation's development. Covering the walls of an open balcony corridor in the palace, Rivera's artwork brings Mexico's history to life, from the enslavement of the Indians to the peasant revolt led by Zapata during the Mexican Revolution.

Cuernavaca's cathedral is a little different from others in the country. Although it was built in the early 1500s, the interior of the building is decidedly modern. Objects that are commonly associated with Mexican cathedrals also adorned this one at one time. Over the years—and a revolution—many of the ornaments were taken and never returned. The *Catedral* does have its beauty, however; one wall contains a mural of missionaries who sailed from Mexico to Japan in the 1500s.

Mexicans believe in the efficacy of herbal medicine, and Cuernavaca has a museum that shows off the power of the plant. Since the time of the Aztecs, herbs have been used to heal wounds and relieve common ailments. Mexicans, who still use traditional teas to settle stomachaches, headaches, and other pains, can purchase many of these herbs in the market. Cuernavaca's *Museum of Herbal and Traditional Medicine,* located at Matamoros 200, displays scores of different plants that are believed to help people get over their sicknesses.

Cuernavaca also has its shopping pleasures, including many of the major department stores. As in most Mexican cities, arts and crafts abound in Cuernavaca and can be purchased at very reasonable prices. Grocery stores and bookstores are common, and English-language publications can be found in most downtown newsstands.

Because of Cuernavaca's attractiveness as a retirement community, there are numerous clubs that cater to residents. The Navy League of the United States and the American Legion Post 10 are active in the community. Clubs such as these serve as gathering points for English-speaking retirees and good sources of information on local events.

▲▲▲

Información Práctica

Population: 500,000.
Altitude: 5,000 feet.
Weather: The temperature is stable throughout the year at about 70 degrees. June to September is the

Cuernavaca

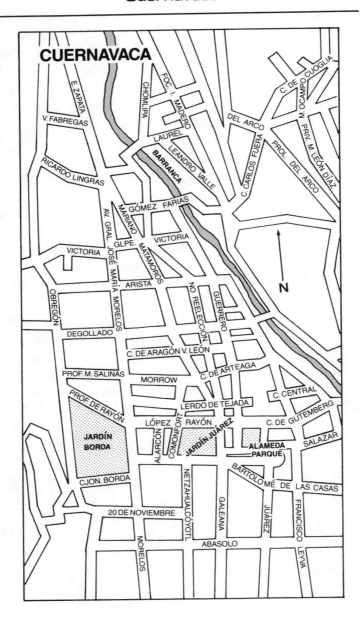

rainy season, but the temperature is still consistently pleasant.

Housing: Because Cuernavaca is the state capital and is close to the nation's capital, housing in the city is more expensive than in other retirement locations. Expect to pay up to $700 a month for a house and about $500 for an apartment.

Golfing: Hacienda de Cocoyoc, located about twenty-five miles from downtown, is a restored sixteenth-century estate that features 9- and 18-hole golf courses (telephone: 12-2000). *San Gaspar,* an 18-hole, 72-par course, is about twenty miles from Cuernavaca in the town of Jicotepec. It is located at Avenida Emiliano Zapata 15, Cliserio Alanís. *Los Tabachines Club de Golf,* the city's newest course, is the site of the annual Cuernavaca Golf Open Tournament in February. It is open to visitors who can demonstrate membership in a U.S. club.

Tennis: Modern tennis courts can be found at many Cuernavaca hotels, such as *El Mirador, Villas del Conquistador,* and *Jacarandas.* The *Cuernavaca Racquet Club* is where the city's upper-class go to play tennis. It features nine tennis courts, as well as a pool and dining facilities. Temporary memberships are available. It is located at Francisco Villa 100 (telephone: 13-0300). *Palace,* which is located at Paseo del Conquistador 903, has four courts. *Villa Internacional de Tenis* on Lomas de Atzingo features eight courts.

Transportation: Driving to Cuernavaca from Mexico City is easily accomplished by following Mexico Highway 95D. The scenic route through the hills surrounding Mexico City also passes a monument to Morelos along the way.

Bus Station: Bus travel to Cuernavaca is excellent. From Mexico City, first-class service, which entitles you to a reserved seat on a good bus, is available from the *Terminal Sur,* located at the Tesqueña Metro stop. The ride from Mexico City to Cuernavaca takes about one hour, and passengers arrive at a downtown bus station, which is located at the corner of Abasolo and Netzahualcoyotl. Service to Taxco, about forty minutes, and Acapulco, about four hours, is also available.

Spas: The "city of eternal spring" would be inappropriately named if it did not have a great spa. The *Villa Vegetariana* combines a diet program with relaxation in warm spas. For information, write to Apartado Postal 1228, Pino 114, Sta. María Ahuacatilan, Cuernavaca, Morelos 62058 (telephone: 313-1044).

Hotels: Las Mañanitas is a Cuernavaca landmark because of its garden restaurant. It features 28 rooms and a pool and is located at Ricardo Linares 107 (telephone: 12-4700). *El Mirador* features 100 rooms, tennis courts, a pool, and a restaurant. It is located on Francisco Villa (telephone: 15-1900). The *OK Inn,* located at Emiliano Zapata 825, features 46 rooms, some with kitchens (telephone: 13-1270).

RV Parks: Monasterio Benedictino Trailer Park is situated on the north side of Cuernavaca on Highway 95D in the village of Ahuatepec, and it has 60 sites. *Cuernavaca Trailer Park,* with 130 sites, is located at Calle Mesalina No. 3 in Colonia Delicias.

Religious Services: Cuernavaca has services for most religions, and some services are in English. Hotel front desks maintain a current listing of churches and temples in their areas and the times of the English services.

Taxco

▼▼

Eighteenth-century Mexico is still alive in Taxco. The white buildings, with terra-cotta tile roofs and flowers balanced on balcony ledges, immediately catch your attention. Well-kept homes and small shops of the local craftsmen hug the cobble-stone streets and charming alleys that run through the city. If you seek quiet colonial living, with a never-ending view of gently rolling hills, then you should consider Taxco.

More than anything, Taxco is synonymous with silver. While small silver veins had been worked by the Indians centuries ago, it was not until the Spaniards arrived that production was expanded. The new owners, who changed the name from the native *Tlachco* to the similar-sounding *Taxco,* continued to discover more lines of silver and other metals in the hills.

Taxco's silver production was steady and profitable. Then, in 1716 a teenage Frenchman named José de la Borda arrived in this hillside village to work as a miner for his brother. De la Borda changed the destiny of Taxco when he struck the mother lode. His discovery of a sea of silver in the hills made Taxco the most important source of *plata* for decades to come.

De la Borda was immensely grateful for the wealth that silver brought to himself and others in Taxco. An inscription on a magnificent church built by the religious de la Borda summarized his contribution: "God gives to Borda, and Borda gives to God." Unfortunately, when he died in 1778, so did Taxco's silver production.

More than a century passed before Taxco awoke from its slumber. An American writer named William Spratling settled down in Taxco in 1929 to work on a book for a U.S. publisher. Unfortunately, the publishing house went out of business.

91

The writer turned to a craft with a long history in Taxco—silversmithing. While Taxco had a good reputation for its silversmith work, Spratling added his own flair to the art and began teaching the craft to other residents. Soon his designs and techniques gained acclaim. Spratling's efforts changed Taxco into the silversmith capital of this hemisphere, and even now his workshop continues to turn out fine pieces of silver.

Like other colonial cities, Taxco is a quaint urban area that attracts tourists from around the world. Fortunately, strict building laws only permit the construction of colonial-style buildings. Because of these rules, Taxco today looks much the same as it did when de la Borda died in 1778 or when Spratling arrived in 1929—colonial, romantic, and inviting.

Despite Taxco's popularity as a tourist attraction, the retirement community remains fairly small. It is a three-hour drive to Mexico City's international airport, which many people who choose to settle in nearby Cuernavaca find inconvenient. Unlike Cuernavaca, Taxco does not have all the amenities, such as large grocery stores or well-known language schools with Spanish classes. They do exist, but on a smaller scale, and require a little determination in finding and utilizing them.

Nevertheless, Taxco is still a charming place in which to retire, and snowbirds do flock to the city. Taxco draws them for one reason: simple living. Taxco is clean, uncrowded, and offers a variety of activities.

Local Sights

It is estimated that the road from Cuernavaca to Taxco has more than 170 curves. Driving to the hillside community is exciting, if not challenging. Along the way children try to sell drivers of passing cars cold refreshments and even iguanas. Passengers in the cars, however, try to save their money for Taxco's silver shops.

In addition to its silver shops and the occasional iguana, Taxco has a unique character to offer retirees. *Santa Prisca,* the local church, built on the zócalo by de la Borda, features two 130-foot towers that rise from the building. The front of the church is carved stone; inside, there are twelve altars and original paintings by colonial painter Miguel Cabrera.

Fiestas are popular in Taxco. In November, a week-long Silver Fair brings out some of the area's best work. During Holy Week, daily parades celebrate Easter, and on the Thursday before Easter the entire city celebrates all day in front of the Santa Prisca church.

▲▲

Información Práctica

Population: 100,000.

Altitude: 5,500 feet.

Weather: Winters are only slightly chilly. Residents usually don sweaters and have their fireplaces going when the evenings become too cool. Throughout the year, daytime temperatures average from 65 to 75 degrees. The rainy season runs from May to August, when monthly precipitation is from three to twelve inches.

Housing: Finding rental property is not easy, but it can be done. People who are familiar with Taxco suggest that you ask everyone you meet about any leads. They claim that this strategy pays off. Rent ranges from $200 to $400 a month. There are retirement housing developments in Taxco, and additional "settlements" are being planned.

Golfing: Colonial Taxco does have its modern advantages. A 9-hole golf course at the hotel *Montetaxco* is located on Route 95 (telephone: 2-1300).

Tennis: Courts can be found at several hotels, including the *Montetaxco.* The hotel *Posada de la Misión* on Avenida John F. Kennedy (telephone: 2-0063) and the *Hacienda del Solar* on the outskirts of Taxco (telephone: 2-0323) have tennis courts.

Spas: There are spas in nearby Cuernavaca. In addition, a spa that can be reached by people living in Taxco is *Ixtapán de la Sal,* which offers tennis and a 9-hole golf course (mailing address: 132 Paseo de la Reforma, México D.F. 06600; telephone: 566-2855).

Transportation: Bus Station: Buses leave from Mexico City and Cuernavaca to Taxco on a regular, daily basis. The bus station is located on the corner of Avenida John F. Kennedy and Calle Reforma.

Hotels: Los Arcos features 30 rooms, a swimming pool, and a restaurant. It is located at Juan Ruiz de Alarcón 12 (telephone: 2-1836). *Hotel Posada de los Castillo,* located at Juan Ruiz de Alarcón 3, has 15 rooms and features a small restaurant (telephone: 2-1396). *Loma Linda* has 90 rooms, a restaurant, and a bar. It is located at Avenida John F. Kennedy 52 (telephone: 2-0206).

RV Park: Loma Linda, a small park that features five sites, is located on Highway 57 (mailing address: Avenida John F. Kennedy No. 54, Taxco, Guerrero).

Mexico City

▼▼▼▼▼▼▼▼▼▼▼▼▼▼▼▼▼▼▼▼▼▼▼▼▼▼▼▼▼▼▼▼▼▼▼▼

opher Columbus set sail for the New World, vas already a bustling center of culture and Aztecs, a powerful tribe known for its legions had well-developed trade routes throughout the country. The Aztec religious leaders and educators had made scientific discoveries that were still unknown in Europe.

Mexico City is a fascinating city that is built on a legend. Aztec leaders, acting on the guidance of their gods, were told to build a new capital. But the gods were very specific about where this city should be constructed. After years of traveling, the Aztecs happened across an eagle that was eating a snake while perched on a cactus in the middle of a lake bed. The demands of the gods were fulfilled, and today that place is Mexico City. While the story is a myth, the eagle, snake, and cactus have become the nation's official emblem.

Modern Mexico City is a town of multiple personalities. The sprawling metropolis offers almost every type of architecture—pre-Columbian, colonial, and modern. Mexico City has also become a mecca for Latin American entertainment, a crossroads for travelers, and a symbol of opportunity for millions of people.

Mexico City's layout could be roughly compared to New York City's boroughs, only a little crazier. Huge Mexico City is made up of *delegaciones,* which are further divided into *colonias.*

San Ángel, for example, is a *colonia* within this gargantuan city that continues to preserve its classic identity and character. San Ángel's narrow cobblestone streets and well-kept colonial buildings are enticing. It is here that Mexican muralist Diego Rivera and his wife Frida Kalo lived and worked; their former residence is now a museum.

San Ángel's beauty and quiet continue to attract Mexico's wealthy and the international community, as well as retirees who make their homes in this colonial ambience. It is here that they enjoy quaint stores, an open market called *Bazaar Sábado,* and a wide variety of restaurants. On the outskirts of San Ángel is a U.S.-affiliated English-language college, Universidad de México, that offers fully accredited courses.

In all honesty, to retire full time in Mexico City requires a special talent. Because of nineteen million residents, traffic congestion, and the continuing uncontrolled urban sprawl, Mexico City should really only be considered by people who truly enjoy large cities. Nevertheless, there are wonderful enclaves, such as San Ángel and Coyoyocán, that offer a retreat from the daily bustle of the nation's capital.

Living in Mexico City may not be for every retiree, but visiting the city is a must. Weekends are the best time for visitors who desire the benefits and excitement of a big city, because many of the city's full-time residents leave town or just stay home, and the metropolis can be successfully managed with less trouble.

Local Sights

Mexico City is a nation unto itself. From shopping in the *Zona Rosa,* which features trendy boutiques and sidewalk cafés, to strolling around the *Zócalo,* Mexico City has something to offer every visitor and resident. Most people who visit the capital never really have a chance to see all of the city, but they can tackle selected areas during their visits.

Mexico City has a wealth of museums that is probably unmatched anywhere in this hemisphere, and maybe in the world. A book could be written about the city's treasure chest of historical displays, but only a few will be highlighted here.

The newest museum is located at the heart of Mexico City on the Zócalo and houses treasures that have been excavated from the *Templo Mayor* (the Great Temple), which was one of the Aztecs' most sacred altars. The *Templo Mayor* was believed to have been destroyed by Hernán Cortés and the Spaniards when they overtook the city, and the stones were allegedly used to build a nearby cathedral.

In 1978, utility workers began excavating the streets around the Zócalo. Their picks and shovels continued to peel away the earth when they began to uncover what appeared to be ancient artifacts near the cathedral. Archeologists were summoned, and they determined the remains to be those of the *Templo Mayor*. Today, hundreds of artifacts have been found and are on display in a beautiful museum named after the great temple.

Overlooking the city is a museum that once was the castle-home of French Emperor Maximilian, who briefly ruled the country before he was executed in 1867. Now the castle is the site of the *National Museum of History*, which displays a variety of paintings and objects of the post-Hispanic period. For people who enjoy jewelry and colonial art, the second floor of the museum has an amazing display.

It is not necessary to venture into a museum because history can be found almost everywhere in Mexico City. The *Pino Suárez Subway Station* displays an authentic Aztec pyramid, which was unearthed by workers who were extending the system. The pyramid has been incorporated into the modern station and is seen by thousands of passersby, as well as tourists.

In the northern section of Mexico City is one of the most religious shrines in this hemisphere—*the Basílica de la Virgen de Guadalupe*. According to the legend, the Virgin Mary appeared before an Indian boy named Juan Diego in 1531 and told him to see that a church was built in her honor. While the local bishop did not believe Juan Diego's story, he later provided proof that convinced authorities. Juan Diego, who had returned to the site and told the Virgin Mary of the bishop's disbelief, was given roses by the Virgin. Juan Diego wrapped the roses in his robe and ran to the bishop. When Juan Diego displayed the flowers, an image of the Virgin was left on his robe.

Two shrines now stand at the site. A new *basílica,* which was opened in 1976, offers religious services, while the older building serves as a museum. The *basílica,* located at the end of Avenida Guadalupe, can be reached by the subway.

▲▲

Información Práctica

Population: 19,000,000.

Altitude: 7,000 feet.

Weather: The rainy season runs from June to August, with an average monthly rainfall of about five inches. In December and January, the nights turn cold (about 45 degrees) but the days warm up to about 65 degrees.

Housing: Moderately priced housing is hard to find; you can expect to pay $600 or more a month. For housing in choice areas, prices run to $1,000 and more a month. *The Mexico City News* has numerous classified ads, with the prices typically listed in U.S. dollars.

Golfing: Mexico City features several fine golf courses: *Bellavista,* located in Ciudad Satélite, in the state of México; *Campestre,* Mexico's oldest operating club; *Chapultepec,* an 18-hole course, located in the southern end of the city at Avenida

Conscripto 425; *La Hacienda,* located in the area of Tlalnepantla in Ciudad Satélite; *Club de Golf de México,* featuring two 18-hole courses and located in the southern area of Tlalpan at Avenida Glorieta Sur 64; and *Vallescondido,* located at Insurgentes Sur 1673.

Tennis: Many hotels have their own private tennis courts, and the golf courses listed above also feature tennis courts. In addition, racquet clubs abound in Mexico City.

Transportation: *Airport:* Benito Juárez International Airport provides service to the United States, Canada, and elsewhere. Domestic flights also depart and arrive at the airport, which is located on the northern side of the city. *Bus Station:* As can be imagined, Mexico City is served by four bus terminals, with each terminal providing service to different areas of the country. The *Terminal Sur,* for example, serves Acapulco, Cuernavaca, Ixtapa-Zihuatanejo, and Taxco. *Trains:* The station, called *Estación Buena Vista,* is located on the north side of Mexico City on Avenida Insurgentes.

Hotels: The *Camino Real,* located at Mariano Escobedo 700, is considered one of the city's premier hotels (telephone: 203-2121). *El Presidente Chapultepec,* a chain purchased by Stouffer in 1989, is a popular hotel that is conveniently located near Mexico City's central park, as well as near museums and restaurants. It is located at Campos Elíseos 218 (telephone: 250-7700). The *Hotel Doral,* located at Sullivan 9, is inexpensive and is within walking distance of the Zona Rosa (telephone: 592-2866).

English-language Bookstores: *American Bookstore,* located at Madero 44, has a large selection

99

of books. *Sanborns* sells English-language magazines, *The Mexico City News,* and many popular books. Street vendors throughout the downtown area also carry the leading news weeklies. Major hotels, such as the Camino Real and the El Presidente, carry select U.S. newspapers, such as *The New York Times* and *USA Today.*

Library: The *Anglo Mexican Library and Information Resource Center* is located at Antonio Caso 127, Colonia San Rafael (telephone: 566-4500). *Benjamin Franklin Library* is located at Londres 16 near the Zona Rosa (telephone: 591-0224).

Religious Services: The following services are available in Mexico City: *Bilingual Christian Fellowship,* Playa Regatas 370, Colonia Reforma Ixtaccíhuatl (telephone: 698-1294); *Capital City Baptist Church,* Calle Sur 138 at Bondojito (telephone: 516-1861); *Christ Church Parish* (Episcopal), Montes Escandinavos 405, Lomas (telephone 520-3763); *Church of Christ Scientist,* Dante 21, Colonia Anzures (telephone: 514-6603); *Church of Jesus Christ of Latter-Day Saints* (Mormon), Guadarrama 115, Lomas de Chapultepec (telephone: 540-2790); and *Union Evangelical Church* (interdenominational), Reforma 1870, Lomas (telephone: 520-0436).

The Beach Life

Retiring on a Mexican beach sounds like the ultimate fantasy. Cold piña coladas, warm sand, and the sounds of the ocean washing up on the beach are inviting to the senses. This is the dream that travel brochures feature. *Vamos a la playa* ("Let's go to the beach"), a Mexican song says, and many retirees are taking the lyrics to heart and heading for Mexico's sun-drenched coasts.

Coastal communities provide certain amenities that are hard to pass up—great beaches, wonderful seafood, and plenty of entertainment. Developers in Pacific coast cities, known as Mexico's "Gold Coast," are building condominiums and developments suitable for retirees. The prices are steep when compared to units located in inland cities because retirees are paying a premium for the sand and surf.

Because of their appeal to international tourists, the popular cities provide many conveniences, such as large airports that handle nonstop flights from the United States and Canada. Cities along the coast are not carbon copies of each other; each community enjoys differences that give it a character of its own.

Critics note, however, that the summers on the beach are often hot and humid, and the winter months bring millions of tourists to these cities. Local entertainment is geared more for the passing tourists—and the prices often reflect that fact. Undaunted, retirees continue to examine the beach life.

Mexico has more than 6,000 miles of coastline. Puerto Vallarta, Acapulco, Ixtapa, and Mazatlán rest on some of the best views along the 2,000 miles of Pacific coastline. On the Caribbean side of Mexico, Veracruz and Cancún have drawn a small number of retirees who flee the winter months in the north. This chapter will focus on retirement cities on the Pacific side, however, since they tend to be more popular with retirees.

Acapulco

Acapulco has a reputation that precedes itself. The jet-set crowd bakes on Acapulco's beaches during the day and parties at night. Tourists venture to this city for great restaurants, popular stores, and the always shining sun. On top of a 130-foot cliff called *La Quebrada,* young men take a moment to pray to the Virgin of Guadalupe, Mexico's patron saint, before leaping into the charging surf below.

Certainly Acapulco caters to tourists, but the city has its share of retirees. Mature residents flock here during the winter months, exchanging the snow of the north for the sun of the south. Through community organizations, such as the Friends of Acapulco, residents are able to keep in touch with each other and to make positive contributions to the city. Golfing and tennis are popular in Acapulco, and many retirees can be found teeing off early in the morning before the heat and humidity set in.

Acapulco's prices reflect the business of tourism. Dining out, water sports, and other tourist activities are readily available, but to partake of them regularly may be out of the price range of many people on a fixed income. Acapulco will continue to draw visitors, so residents have to be prepared for crowds during the high season. Nonetheless, many retirees enjoy Acapulco.

Another Acapulco

The hotel strip and beaches receive the most attention, but other parts of Acapulco also hold treasures for visitors. "Old" Acapulco, the colonial section of the city, is where the seeds of modern Acapulco were planted centuries ago.

The *zócalo* is usually abuzz with busy people who are dining in the restaurants and shopping in the stores and boutiques. In *El Mercado Municipal,* for example, a person can purchase most products, from the staples of daily living to unusual trinkets that serve no real purpose but are interesting nonetheless.

Overlooking the city is the *Fuerte de San Diego,* originally built in 1616 to protect Acapulco from pirates, now it stands ready to greet visitors. The fort is the site of the *Museo Histórico de Acapulco,* which features a fine exhibit that charts the city from prehistoric times through Independence in 1821. The museum, which is affiliated with Mexico City's famous Museum of Anthropology, also features touring exhibits.

Gateway to the Orient

While Acapulco is a top spot for tourism today, it has always attracted people. Spanish conquistador Hernán Cortés arrived in what was a small fishing village in 1530 and transformed it into a port that linked Mexico to the Orient. Besides trade, Acapulco played a vital role in Spain's conquest of the Philippines, as galleons left from the port on their way to Manila.

Acapulco was on the move, with much of the commerce revolving around shipping. The wave of prosperity abruptly ended in 1818 during a battle for Mexican independence. Although the battle was short-lived, Acapulco lapsed into a coma for more than one hundred years.

During and after World War II, Acapulco began to grow again. President Miguel Alemán Valdés, who took office in 1946, laid out aggressive tourism plans for the city that included putting in water and sewers, paving the streets, and opening up the city to travelers. President Alemán's renovations helped to stir interest among Mexican travelers and a few visitors from the United States. While the average tourist helped to build the economy of this coastal community, it was the Hollywood crowd that gave it a world reputation in the late 1940s and 1950s.

Acapulco's growth continued almost unabated. Fiestas, water sports, and cruise ships ladened with passengers helped to perpetuate Acapulco's image as a party town. With fame as a popular tourist destination, however, the community's leaders did not want the city to lose its charm for the residents. The city square was renovated in the 1980s, and hotels and other establishments have been pushed to keep their areas clean and inviting.

Acapulco

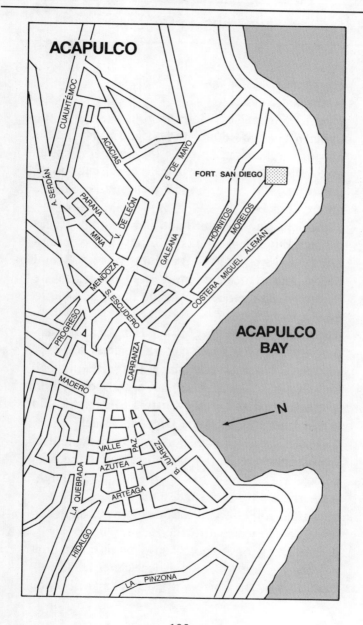

ACAPULCO

FORT SAN DIEGO

COSTERA MIGUEL ALEMÁN

HORNITOS

MORELOS

CUAUHTÉMOC

ACACIAS

5 DE MAYO

A. SERDÁN

PARANA

V. DE LEÓN

MINA

GALEANA

MENDOZA

S. ESCUDERO

PROGRESO

CARRANZA

MADERO

**ACAPULCO
BAY**

N

VALLE

AZUTEA

LA PAZ

JUAREZ

LA QUEBRADA

ARTEAGA

HIDALGO

LA PINZONA

105

▲▲▲

Información Práctica

Population: 1,000,000.

Altitude: Sea level.

Weather: Acapulco's winter months average in the upper 70s and low 80s, with no significant rainfall. During the summer, however, the weather is hotter and more humid. June can receive as much as 17 inches of rain; July, about 9 inches; and August, about 10 inches.

Housing: Condominiums and single-family homes can be found in Acapulco. Oceanside condominiums, however, carry premium prices. Rental homes and apartments away from the beach are relatively more moderate, in the range of $400 to $700 a month.

Museums: Besides the *Museo Histórico de Acapulco,* the city has a nice cultural center. Called the *Centro Cultural de Acapulco,* it is a series of small buildings that includes a small anthropology museum. It is located on the Costera Miguel Alemán across from the Acapulco Dolphins Hotel.

Golfing: There are three golf courses in Acapulco. Two championship, 18-hole courses are at the Acapulco Princess and the Pierre Marques hotels. Both hotels are on the road to the airport. A 9-hole municipal golf course is located on the Costera Miguel Alemán in front of the Elcano Hotel.

Tennis: Many of the hotels have tennis courts that visitors can use for a small fee. *Club de Tenis y Golf,* located on Costera Miguel Alemán, is open to guests. *Tiffany's Racquet Club,* at Avenida Villa Vera 120, has five courts.

Transportation: *Airport:* The international airport is about 25 minutes from the center of Acapulco; vans provide inexpensive transportation to hotels. Taxis are also available. International airline flights into Acapulco are a daily experience, but the airport remains relatively small and is easy to get around.

Bus Station: It is about a six-hour trip from Mexico City's Central de Autobuses del Sur to Acapulco's station located at Calles Cuauhtémoc and Magallanes.

Hotels: Acapulco has a collection of hotels that ranges from the internationally known Hyatt to small family-run establishments. A hotel near the beach is the *Acapulco Imperial,* located at Avenida Costera Miguel Alemán 251 (telephone: 5-1759). Some of the older hotels located away from the beach offer lower prices. Near the main plaza is the *Hotel Angelita,* at Quebrada 37, that has reasonably priced rooms featuring ceiling fans and private bathrooms (telephone: 3-5734).

RV Parks: *Acapulco Trailer Park,* located on the Pie de la Cuesta beach, has 60 sites and offers boating facilities (mailing address: Apartado Postal 1, Acapulco, Guerrero). *El Coloso,* located on Highway 200 east just off Highway 95, has 150 sites. *La Roca,* located about three miles from El Coloso on Highway 200, is a small park with 20 sites. *Quinta Dora Trailer Park,* which has 14 sites, is located north of Acapulco on Highway 200.

Religious Services: Hotels can provide you with schedules of local religious services.

Mazatlán

▼▼▼

Resting on a peninsula, Mazatlán is a paradise for sun lovers and deep-sea anglers. Mazatlán is set against a backdrop of three large hills that run from the peninsula's tip to an area well beyond the north of the city's center. Mazatlán's reputation for clean beaches, stable climate, and international accessibility have made it an attractive haven for people fleeing the northern winters.

Mazatlán rests just south along an imaginary line called the Tropic of Cancer, the official boundary that marks the northern edge of the tropics. There are very noticeable differences on either side of this line: north of the Tropic of Cancer are drier lands, where rainfall in the summer is slight; south of it, the weather is wet throughout the year, which helps to produce the lush vegetation that people commonly associate with tropical climates.

Mazatlán is in an ideal situation, since it reaps the benefits of both sides of the Tropic of Cancer. Rainfall is sufficient to produce the greenery that gives the countryside splashes of color, while the northern drier influences help reduce the humidity.

Mazatlán is known in Mexico for more than its wonderful climate, for it is also rich in history that people would expect to read in stirring sea novels. Centuries ago, pirates preyed on Spanish ships loaded with mineral wealth from the cities of Rosario and Panuco. They would hide their plundered wealth along the Mexican beaches to be retrieved at a later date.

U.S. warships formed a blockade around the port in 1847 in preparation for an American invasion during the Mexican-American War. French warships took up a blockade around the city in 1864, and the residents surrendered to the Napoleonic forces after being bombarded.

Record-setting Marlin and Other Attractions

Mazatlán is a peaceful community of more than 700,000 people. Commercial fishermen in the area bring in the nation's largest catches of shrimp, which are packed locally (but far from tourist areas) and then distributed throughout the country and the United States.

Mazatlán continues to be a draw for sport fishermen, as well. Marlin and other sailfish can be caught throughout the year in the waters off Mazatlán. In fact, the record-setting black marlin (12 feet at 988 pounds) was caught off its shores in 1980. Eight fleets of charter boats take visiting anglers to some of the best fishing spots, where more than 5,000 billfish are reportedly caught each year.

Mazatlán also has a nationwide reputation for its *Carnaval,* which takes place the week before Lent begins. Mazatlán's *Carnaval* features the coronation of a queen, parades, parties, and a host of other activities. In the evenings, mariachis stroll the streets playing for the many outdoor parties.

Despite its history and color, Mazatlán does not have all the colonial charms of other towns like Guadalajara or Puerto Vallarta. There are nearby colonial towns, such as Concordia and Rosario, that can be explored during day trips.

In Mazatlán, snowbirds are more common than full-time retired residents. Condominium developments and the easy accessibility for people who live in California, Oregon, and Washington, make Mazatlán an ideal get-away city. The numbers of tourists and snowbirds, however, do not squeeze out full-time retirees. Whether full- or part-time, residents can enjoy golfing and other sports, as well as participation in local social clubs.

Mazatlán

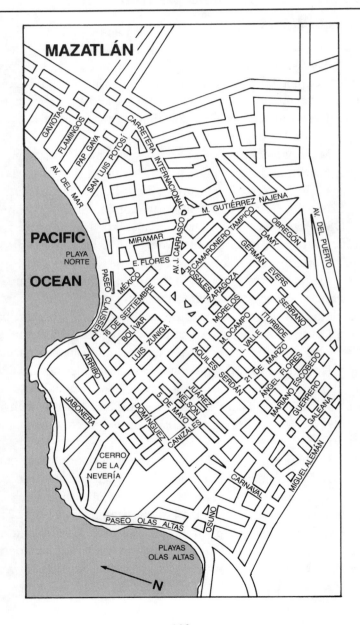

▲▲

Información Práctica

Population: 700,000.

Altitude: Sea level.

Weather: Situated slightly south of the Tropic of Cancer, Mazatlán enjoys "comfortable" beach weather. During the winter months, the daytime temperature stays in the 70-degree range. In the summer, the daytime temperature stays in the 80s. Rainfall is heaviest during June (1 inch), July (8 inches), August (9 inches), and September (10 inches).

Housing: New condominiums are being added to the existing housing stock. Typical housing prices begin at about $400 a month.

Golfing: El Cid Golf and Country Club is an 18-hole course located on Avenida Camarón Sábalo (telephone: 3-333). *Club Campestre de Mazatlán,* located on Avenida Internacional, features a 9-hole course (telephone: 2-5702).

Tennis: Las Gaviotas Racquet Club has six courts. Many of the hotels feature tennis courts, as does the *El Cid Golf and Country Club.*

Transportation: Airport: The international airport is 14 miles from Mazatlán, and it has several car-rental offices in the terminal. *Bus Station:* Buses arrive and depart from the *Central de Autobuses,* which is located on the Bulevar de Las Américas and Calle Tamazula. *Trains:* There are two trains from Guadalajara to Mazatlán, a ride that takes about eleven hours. *Ferryboat:* Mazatlán can be reached by ferryboat from La Paz in Baja California Sur. The trip across the Sea of Cortez takes sixteen hours, and the ferryboat has private and semi-private cabins.

Hotels: Mazatlán features a variety of hotels in various price ranges. The *Hotel Zaragoza,* located at Zaragoza 18, features 40 rooms with bathrooms and room fans; prices are less than $10 a night (telephone: 678-1-2343).

RV Parks: Las Palmas Trailer Camp is situated in the Zona Dorada area of Mazatlán and offers 65 hookups (mailing address: Camarón Sábalo 333, Apartado Postal 1032, Mazatlán, Sinaloa). *La Posta Trailer Park,* located in downtown Mazatlán, features 200 sites. *Mar Rosa Trailer Park* has 70 hookups right along the beach by the Holiday Inn (mailing address: Camarón Sábalo 333, Apartado Postal 435, Mazatlán). *Maravillas,* located on the beach, is a small campground with 26 sites. *Playa Escondida,* located on the north side of Mazatlán, has 200 sites (mailing address: Apartado Postal 682, Mazatlán, Sinaloa). *San Bartolo* is on the north side of Mazatlán and has 48 sites.

Puerto Vallarta

▼▼▼▼▼▼▼▼▼▼▼▼▼▼▼▼▼▼▼▼▼▼▼▼▼▼▼▼▼▼▼▼▼▼

While Acapulco has become known for its modern tourist developments, Puerto Vallarta has managed to keep its historical flavor. With cobblestone streets and red-tile roof buildings, Puerto Vallarta is working to maintain its image as a charming village while it satisfies the demands of an international tourist market. Strict local building laws, which prohibit high-rise buildings, ensures that the view of the mountains and city remains unspoiled.

When it comes to tourism, Puerto Vallarta is a newcomer. Lacking a fully functioning airport and a superhighway, "PV," as many residents refer to it, was isolated from the rest of the country until the early 1960s. Some people say it was the movie, *Night of the Iguana,* that drew attention to the city. Others say it was the natural expansion of tourism that put Puerto Vallarta on the map. Nonetheless, it seems that the city wants to maintain its traditional charm.

Part of the tourist market has gone to Nuevo Vallarta, which is about eight miles north of Puerto Vallarta. In Nuevo Vallarta developers have constructed tourist complexes that include condominiums, golf courses, tennis courts, and other facilities.

The absence of urban sprawl has helped to keep Puerto Vallarta a manageable city in which to travel. The city is cut in half by the Río Cuale. The main commercial district with its restaurants and hotels lies north of the river.

The Río Cuale sports an island that is complete with restaurants and souvenir stands. On the island, tourists may go for a casual walk, do a little shopping, and enjoy the picturesque view of Puerto Vallarta. Off the island is a wonderful beachfront walkway called the *Malecón*. Strolling along the Malecón, pedestrians can check out the hotels, night clubs, and restaurants, as well as the tourists.

Like Mazatlán and Acapulco, Puerto Vallarta offers residents and visitors a chance to go fishing. Puerto Vallarta has a well-equipped fleet of charter boats that could satisfy most fishing enthusiasts. Yet, anglers do not necessarily have to venture from shore to catch fish. Casting in the Bay of Banderas, fishermen can bring in small tunas and other saltwater fish. Hunting is also possible near Puerto Vallarta; visitors may obtain information from local hotels. Expeditions for deer, wildcat, duck, and quail can be arranged during the months of November to June.

Puerto Vallarta is within driving distance of Guadalajara. Buses leave daily from Guadalajara to Puerto Vallarta; however, the five-hour trip can easily be made in a personal car. It is common for residents in Guadalajara to journey to Puerto Vallarta for a vacation that includes a dip in the ocean and a meal of fresh seafood.

▲▲

Información Práctica

Population: 300,000.

Altitude: Sea level.

Weather: Expect rain in the summer, with July and August each receiving more than four inches of precipitation. Temperatures are fairly steady throughout the year at about 75 degrees, again with increasing temperatures during the summer months.

Housing: Condominiums are available in Puerto Vallarta. There is housing north of the Río Cuale.

Golfing: An 18-hole course called *Los Flamingos* is located in Nuevo Vallarta (telephone: 2-0959).

Tennis: Many of the hotels have tennis courts.

Transportation: Airport: Flying is the most popular method of reaching Puerto Vallarta. Taxis are available to and from the airport, and the price is about $5 to $7. *Bus Station:* Buses arrive on Avenida Insurgentes between the streets of Río Cuale and Serdán.

114

Puerto Vallarta

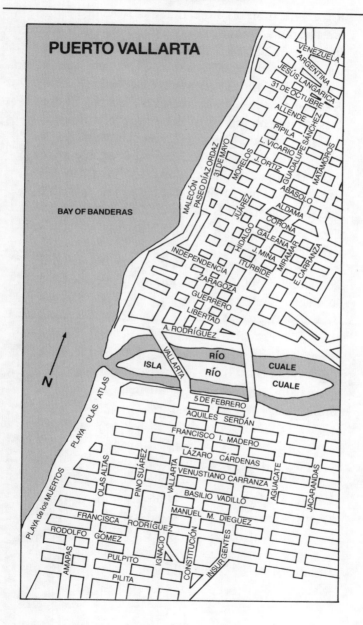

Hotels: Nuevo Hotel Rosita, located north of the Río Cuale, is an old hotel that has remained popular. It has a swimming pool and a view of the ocean (telephone: 2-1033). *Hotel Azteca,* located at Francisco I. Madero 473, has a courtyard and 47 rooms, some with kitchenettes (telephone: 2-2750).

RV Parks: Puerto Vallarta Trailer Park has 70 sites. It is located on the north side of town (mailing address: Apartado Postal 141, Puerto Vallarta, Jalisco). *Tacho's* features 155 sites; it is located across from the marina on the north side of town. *Bucerías,* which has 55 sites, is about 15 miles north of Puerto Vallarta on Highway 200. *La Martoca Bungalows,* also 15 miles north of the city on Highway 200, has five sites.

Religious Services: A listing of current religious services in English can be obtained from the hotels in Puerto Vallarta.

9

Mexico: Resources

▲▲
▽▽

T his chapter will help you get started on your quest to relocating or retiring in paradise. You will find the following sections to be useful in doing your preliminary background work, as well as in making contacts once you are in sunny Mexico: Publications and Organizations for a wide variety of needs, including camping, handicapped travel, social services, land searches, and daily comforts; Major Holidays and Festivals; Mexican Consular Offices in the United States; Mexican Government Tourism Offices; and U.S. Embassy and Consulate Offices in Mexico.

Publications and Organizations

▼▼▼▼▼▼▼▼▼▼▼▼▼▼▼▼▼▼▼▼▼▼▼▼▼▼▼▼▼▼▼▼▼▼▼▼▼▼

A successful trip to Mexico will require a little homework on your part prior to departure. A wide selection of information can be obtained by contacting organizations in the United States and Mexico, and this listing may help you to find out more about Mexico before, during, and after your exploratory visits.

Camping and Recreational Vehicles

Mexico Camping Directory is a comprehensive guide to where to pitch your tent. It lists campgrounds, restaurants, and fishing camps; it also contains useful maps. Travelmex, Apartado Postal 31-750, Guadalajara, Jalisco.

RV Park & Campground Directory 1990 by the Allstate Motor Club is a complete list of facilities in the United States, Canada, and Mexico. It is published by Prentice Hall.

The People's Guide to RV Camping in Mexico, by Carl Franz with Steve Rogers, is a how-to book that includes a comprehensive directory of campgrounds in Mexico. John Muir Publications, P.O. Box 613, Santa Fe, NM 87504.

Handicapped Travel

Access to Travel: A Guide to the Accessibility of Airport Terminals is a free publication that reviews more than 400 airports in 42 countries on 70 features, such as restrooms and corridor widths. Airport Operators Council International, 1220 19th St., NW, Washington, D.C. 20036. Telephone: (202) 293-8500.

Disabled Traveler's International Phrasebook contains useful phrases in Spanish. It is published by Disability Press Ltd., 17 Union St., Kingston-on-Thames, Surrey KT1 1RP.

"Incapacitated Passengers' Air Travel Guide," published by the International Air Transport Association (IATA), is a free brochure that explains arrangements that can be made and how to go about making them. IATA, 2000 Peel St., Montreal, Quebec H3A 2R4.

Information Center for Individuals with Disabilities publishes information on travel professionals and resources for handicapped persons. ICID, 27-43 Wormwood, Boston, MA 02210. Telephone: (617) 727-5540. Fee: Free for residents of Massachusetts; $5 for nonresidents.

Mobility International/USA offers advice and assistance to handicapped travelers. It publishes a quarterly newsletter and sourcebook. MIUSA, P.O. Box 3551, Eugene, OR 97403. Telephone: (503) 343-1284. Membership: $20 annually.

Society for the Advancement of Travel for the Handicapped publishes a quarterly newsletter and provides information on travel professionals who have experience in helping handicapped travelers. SATH, 26 Court St., Penthouse Suite, Brooklyn, NY 11242. Telephone: (718) 858-5483.

Travel Information Service provides information on handicapped travel in countries around the world and it provides toll-free telephone numbers for airlines that have equipment for the hearing-impaired. Moss Rehabilitation Hospital, 1200 West Tabor Rd., Philadelphia, PA 19141-3099. Telephone: (215) 329-5715. Fee: $5 for information on three cities.

Helpful Organizations in Mexico

American-Canadian Club provides residents and those considering living in Mexico up-to-date information. Seminars and newsletters are sponsored by the club. Address: c/o Hotel Vista Plaza del Sol, Avenida López Mateos and Mariano Otero, Guadalajara, Jalisco.

AM-MEX Social Club is a Guadalajara-based organization that sponsors monthly dances and get-togethers. Started in 1988, founders sought to offer residents additional avenues to meet other people. AM-MEX Social Club, Apartado Postal 5-742, Guadalajara, Jalisco.

American Society of Jalisco, founded more than 40 years ago, sponsors cultural and social activities, provides special services, and raises money for local charities. A bulletin board in its offices displays useful information on local events and housing. AmSoc, Apartado Postal 5-510, Colonia Chapalita, Guadalajara, Jalisco. Membership: $20 individual, $25 family annually.

Fellowship for UNOS is a Guadalajara support group for people who live alone. Its weekly meetings are listed in *The Mexico City News.*

Friends of Acapulco, founded more than 30 years ago, is a civic and social organization. Among its many activities, members help raise funds for five local orphanages, a medical clinic, and a scholarship program. Friends of Acapulco, Apartado Postal C-64, Acapulco, Guerrero 39670. Telephone: 5-02-55.

Lake Chapala Society is a community organization in Ajijic. It is located at 16 de Septiembre No. 16, Ajijic, Jalisco.

Newcomers Club is a Mexico City-based organization that conducts monthly meetings with new arrivals. Its meetings are held on the second Friday of each month at the Union Church, Paseo de la Reforma 1870, Colonia Lomas, Mexico City.

Retiring in Guadalajara is an advisory organization that maintains a clearinghouse of material on living in Mexico. These materials, which include maps and "Maid in Spanish," are available for sale. Fran and Judy Furton, Apartado Postal 5-409, Guadalajara, Jalisco. Telephone: 21-23-48.

Helpful U.S. Organizations

American Association of Retired Persons' $5 annual membership fee entitles people age 50 and older to become part of the Purchase Privilege program. In addition, AARP maintains a listing of information on retiring in Mexico. AARP, 1909 K St., NW, Washington, D.C. 20049. Telephone: (202) 872-4700.

Elderhostel has language and cultural programs in Mexico. A program catalogue is available. Elderhostel, 80 Boylston St., Suite 400, Boston, MA 02116. Telephone: (617) 426-7788.

The Friendship Force offers one-week exchange programs around the world, including Mexico. The Friendship Force, 575 CNN Center, Atlanta, GA 30303. Telephone: (404) 522-9490.

Golden Companions provides members with a bimonthly newsletter, vacation-home listing, travel information, and more. Golden Companions, P.O. Box 754, Pullman, WA 99163. Membership: $48.

Language Study Abroad is a program that caters to senior citizens. Language Study Abroad, 1301 North Maryland Ave., Glendale, CA 91207. Telephone: (818) 242-5263.

Mature Outlook provides discounts on hotels and travel for people age 50 and older. Mature Outlook, Inc., Allstate Plaza, Northbrook, IL 60062. Telephone: (708) 402-7800.

Mexico Retirement and Travel Assistance is an independent organization that has materials, including a book and videotape, on living in Mexico. MRTA, P.O. Box 2190, Henderson, NV 89009.

People to People International, which has two chapters in Mexico, is a cultural exchange program. People to People International, 1501 East Armour Blvd., Kansas City, MO 64109. Telephone: (816) 531-4701.

U.S. Servas Committee is a cultural exchange
program. U.S. Servas Committee, 11 John St., Room
706, New York, NY 10038. Telephone: (212) 267-0252.

Publications

AIM, Adventures in Mexico is a six-issues-a-year
newsletter that keeps readers up to date on various
retiree locations in Mexico, including information on
housing, prices, and population. This is an excellent
publication for tracking the changing nature of
retirement in Mexico. *AIM,* Apartado Postal 31-70,
Guadalajara, Jalisco 45050. Price: $15 annually.

Atención San Miguel, published by local volunteers, is
a weekly hometown paper full of fun and information
for the artistic community of San Miguel de Allende.
Articles on real estate, advice columns, and meeting
notices are usually included. *Atención,* Biblioteca
Pública, Apartado Postal 119, San Miguel de Allende,
Gto. Price: $30 annually.

Baja Traveler is a quarterly magazine that focuses on
this wonderful area of Mexico. While it is geared
more for the sportsman or outdoor person, it is
wonderful reading. *Baja,* c/o Topography
International, Inc., 304 S. Chestnut St., P.O. Box 908,
Henderson, NC 27565. Price: $8.

The Colony Reporter is a weekly newspaper that is a
key source of information on Mexico's most popular
retirement location—Guadalajara. *The Colony
Reporter,* Duque de Rivas 254, Guadalajara, Jalisco
44140. Telephone: 52-21-77. Price: $45 annually.

The Mexico City News is a staple for the English-speaking community in Mexico. The newspaper contains local, national, and international news, as well as many of the syndicated features that people have come to love back home. Most important it contains extensive classified advertisements. *The News,* Balderas 87, 3 Piso, México, D. F. 06050. Telephone: 521-08-88. Price: $30 for six months.

PV. Puerto Vallarta is a monthly publication on this beach community. *PV,* Comunicación Editorial, 28 de Enero 339 S.R., Guadalajara, Jalisco 44400.

Travelers Guide to Mexico is an annual English-language book that is placed in thousands of hotel rooms around the nation. It provides information on popular cities and activities. Prometur, S.A. de C.V., Gral. Juan Cano 68, San Miguel Chapultepec, México, D. F. 11850. Telephone: (525) 515-0925.

Recreation

Mexico West Travel Club, 242 Newport Blvd., Costa Mesa, CA 92627. Sends members a monthly newsletter, fishing reports, and a discount card.

Related Resources

Distant Neighbors is a compelling look at Mexico, its people, and its relationship with the United States. Written by the *New York Times'* former Mexico City Bureau Chief Alan Riding, it is on the must-read list of people wanting a concise look at the nation. Vintage Press, 1984.

The Hispanic Way, by Judith Noble and Jaime Lacasa presents 73 key aspects of Hispanic behavior, attitudes, customs, and culture in a handy A-Z format. Passport Books, 1991.

Labyrinth of Solitude: Life and Thought in Mexico, by Octavio Paz, is considered essential reading for all students of Mexico. Grove Press, 1962.

Limits of Friendship takes an analytical look at how the United States and Mexico view each other. Public policy issues are analyzed by a Mexican, Jorge Casteñada, and an American, Robert Pastor. Alfred A. Knopf, 1989.

Title Search

International Land Title Insurance is a company that investigates deeds and reports on whether a piece of property can be sold. United States office: 6032 Lake Worth Blvd., Fort Worth, TX 76135; telephone: (817) 237-5000. Mexico office: Parral No. 6, Esq. J. Escutia, Colonia Condesa, México, D. F. 06140; telephone: (525) 211-6686.

Major Holidays and Festivals

▼▼

Some people joke that Mexico has more holidays than any other nation. Whether or not the final count puts Mexico in the lead, Mexicans find many occasions for celebration. Incidentally, if a holiday falls on a Thursday or a Tuesday, many Mexicans will take what is called a *puente* (bridge). Essentially, this means that people take off the Friday or Monday in addition to the holiday, which gives them a long weekend. The following is a list of the major holidays and festivals:

January 1: New Year's Day, a legal holiday.

January 6: Three Kings' Day, also known as the Wise Men's Day. Children receive presents as children do in the U.S. on Christmas Day.

January 17: The Feast of St. Antony, the Abbott, is celebrated by the blessing of animals.

February 2: Candlemas Day is celebrated throughout Mexico. In Salvatierra, Guanajuato, there is a fair that features rides and fireworks.

February 5: Constitution Day, a legal holiday, is celebrated with official ceremonies.

February 13: Carnival is celebrated in major coastal cities, such as Veracruz and Mazatlán, with floats, music, and dancing.

March or April *(varies):* Holy Week, also known as *Semana Santa,* is celebrated with religious processions and ceremonies.

March 21: Celebration of Benito Juárez's birthday, a legal holiday. The former president is known as "the Abraham Lincoln of Mexico."

May 1: Labor Day, a legal holiday.

May 5: *Cinco de Mayo,* the celebration of the Mexican victory over the French troops encamped in Puebla.

August 15: Assumption Day is celebrated. In Huamantla, Tlaxcala, more than three miles of floral carpets are laid out, over which the figure of the Virgin of Guadalupe is carried.

September 15: *El Grito,* the yell, is celebrated at 11 P.M. This is the start of Independence Day, which is symbolized by the president stepping out onto the balcony of the Presidential Palace in Mexico City's Zócalo and ringing the national bell.

September 16: Independence Day.

October *(varies):* International Cerventino Festival in Guanajuato, which features music, theater, and dance from around the world.

October *(varies):* October Festival in Guadalajara, which is the state's answer to Octoberfest.

November 2: Day of the Dead. This is a major religious holiday in Mexico.

November *(varies):* National Silver Fair, Taxco. This one-week celebration allows Taxcans to display their skills and wares of silversmithing.

December 8: Feast of the Immaculate Conception is celebrated, particularly in Morelia, where the city is transformed into a fairyland of color, lights, and flowers.

December 12: Mexico's patron saint, Our Lady of Guadalupe, is celebrated.

December 16: The start of Mexico's *Posadas,* the traditional celebration before Christmas. This is a popular time for parties.

December 25: Christmas Day.

Mexican Consular Offices in the United States

▼▼▼▼▼▼▼▼▼▼▼▼▼▼▼▼▼▼▼▼▼▼▼▼▼▼▼▼▼▼▼▼▼▼▼▼▼▼

Mexican Consular Offices provide information on traveling in Mexico. People applying for FM-3 and FM-2 visas will need to have their translated documents certified by the nearest Mexican Consular Office.

Alabama

Mobile: Gastelum Enrique Gómez Palcio, 801 Sullivan Ave., Mobile, AL 36609. Telephone: (205) 653-4560.

Arizona

Nogales: 135 Terrace Ave., Nogales, AZ 85621. Telephone: (602) 287-2521.

Phoenix: 700 East Jefferson, Suite 150, Phoenix, AZ 85034. Telephone: (602) 242-7398.

Tucson: 553 South Stone Ave., Tucson, AZ 85701. Telephone: (602) 882-5595.

California

Calexico: 331 West Second St., Calexico, CA 92231. Telephone: (619) 357-3863.

Fresno: 2839 Mariposa St., Fresno, CA 93721. Telephone: (209) 233-3065.

Los Angeles: 125 East Paseo de la Plaza, Los Angeles, CA 90012. Telephone: (213) 624-3261.

Oxnard: 201 East Fourth St., Oxnard, CA 93030. Telephone: (805) 483-4684.

Sacramento: 9845 Horn Road, Suite 120, Sacramento, CA 95814. Telephone: (916) 363-0801.

San Bernardino: 588 West Sixth St., San Bernardino, CA 92401. Telephone: (714) 889-9836.

San Diego: 610 "A" St., Suite 100, San Diego, CA 92101. Telephone: (619) 231-8414.

San Francisco: 870 Market St., Suite 528, San Francisco, CA 94102. Telephone: (415) 392-5554.

San José: 380 North First St., San José, CA 95113. Telephone: (408) 294-3414.

Santa Ana: 406 West Fourth St., Santa Ana, CA 92701. Telephone: (714) 835-3069.

Colorado

Denver: 707 Washington St., Suite "A," Denver, CO 80203. Telephone: (303) 830-0601.

Florida

Miami: 780 N.W. Le Jeune Road, Suite 525, Miami, FL 33145. Telephone: (305) 441-8780.

Tampa: 1717 West Cass St., Box 1790, Tampa, FL 33606. Telephone: (813) 223-1481.

Georgia

Atlanta: 410 South Center, One CNN Center, Atlanta, GA 30303-2705. Telephone: (404) 688-3258.

Hawaii

Honolulu: 2828 Paa St., Suite 2150, Honolulu, HI 96819. Telephone: (808) 833-6331.

Illinois

Chicago: 300 North Michigan Ave., Second Floor, Chicago, IL 60601. Telephone: (312) 855-1380.

Louisiana

New Orleans: World Trade Center Blvd., Suite 1140, Two Canal St., New Orleans, LA 70130. Telephone: (504) 522-3596.

Massachusetts

Boston: 20 Park Plaza, Suite 321, Boston, MA 02116.
Telephone: (617) 426-8782.

Michigan

Detroit: 1515 Book Bldg., Washington Blvd. at West
Grand River, Detroit, MI 48226. Telephone: (313)
965-1868.

Minnesota

Rochester: 3 First Ave., SW, Rochester, MN 55901.
Telephone: (507) 288-3130.

Missouri

St. Louis: 1015 Locust St., Suite 922, St. Louis, MO
63101. Telephone: (314) 436-3233.

New Mexico

Albuquerque: 401 Fifth St., NW, Albuquerque, NM
87102. Telephone: (505) 247-2139.

New York

Buffalo: 1875 Harlem Rd., Buffalo, NY 10423.
Telephone: (716) 895-9800.

New York: 8 East 41st St., New York, NY 10017.
Telephone: (212) 689-0456.

North Carolina

Charlotte: 4101 West Blvd., Box 19404, Charlotte, NC 28219. Telephone: (704) 394-2190.

Oregon

Portland: 545 NE 47th Ave., Suite 317, Portland, OR 97213. Telephone: (503) 233-5662.

Pennsylvania

Philadelphia: 575 Bourse Building, 21 South Fifth St., Philadelphia, PA 19106. Telephone: (215) 922-4262.

Puerto Rico

San Juan: The Executive Bldg., Suite 305, Av. Ponce de León 623, San Juan, PR 00918. Telephone: (809) 764-8935.

Tennessee

Nashville: 226 Capitol Blvd., Suite 514, Nashville, TN 37219. Telephone: (605) 244-7430.

Texas

Austin: 200 East Sixth St., Suite 200, Austin, TX 78701. Telephone: (512) 478-2866.

Brownsville: 724 Elizabeth & Seventh Sts., P.O. Box 1711, Brownsville, TX 78520. Telephone: (512) 542-4431.

Corpus Christi: 800 North Shoreline, Corpus Christi, TX 78401. Telephone: (512) 882-3375.

Dallas: 1349 Empire Central, Suite 100, Dallas, TX 75247. Telephone: (214) 630-7341.

Del Rio: 1010 South Main St., Del Rio, TX 78840. Telephone: (512) 775-2352.

Eagle Pass: 140 Adams St., Eagle Pass, TX 78852. Telephone: (512) 773-9255.

El Paso: 910 East San Antonio St., P.O. Box 812, El Paso, TX 79901. Telephone: (915) 533-3644.

Fort Worth: One Commerce Plaza, Fort Worth, TX 76102. Telephone: (817) 335-5691.

Houston: 4200 Montrose Blvd., Suite 120, Houston, TX 77006. Telephone: (713) 524-2300.

Laredo: 1612 Farragut St., P.O. Box 659, Laredo, TX 78040. Telephone: (512) 723-6360.

McAllen: 1418 Beech St., Suite 102, McAllen, TX 78501. Telephone: (512) 686-0243.

Midland: 511 West Ohio, Suite 121, Midland, TX 79701. Telephone: (915) 687-2334.

San Antonio: 127 Navarro St., San Antonio, TX 78205. Telephone: (512) 227-9145.

Utah

Salt Lake City: 182 South 600 East, Suite 202, Salt Lake City, UT 84102. Telephone: (801) 521-8502.

Virginia

Norfolk: 35121 East Virginia Beach Blvd., Suite E-2, Norfolk, VA 23502. Telephone: (804) 461-4553.

Richmond: 2420 Pemberton Rd., Richmond, VA 23229. Telephone: (804) 747-9200.

Washington

Seattle: 2132 Third Ave., Seattle, WA 98121. Telephone: (206) 448-3526.

Spokane: 12005 East Sprague Ave., Spokane, WA 99214. Telephone: (509) 926-4713.

Washington, D.C.

Embassy of Mexico, 1900 Pennsylvania Ave., NW, Washington, D.C. 20006. Telephone: (202) 728-1600.

Wisconsin

Madison: 1818 Fordem Ave. 6, Madison, WI 53704. Telephone: (608) 249-5201.

Mexican Government Tourism Offices

▼▼▼

Mexico has five regional tourism offices in the United States that provide travel information and answer basic immigration questions, among other activities.

California

10100 Santa Monica Blvd., Suite 224, Los Angeles, CA 90067. Telephone: (213) 203-8191.

Illinois

70 East Lake St., Suite 1413, Chicago, IL 60601. Telephone: (312) 565-2786.

New York

405 Park Ave., Suite 1002, New York, NY 10022. Telephone: (212) 755-7261.

Texas

2707 North Loop West, Suite 1413, Houston, TX 77008. Telephone: (713) 880-5131.

Washington, D.C.

1911 Pennsylvania Ave., NW, Washington, D.C. 20006. Telephone: (202) 759-1750.

U.S. Embassy and Consulates in Mexico

▼▼▼▼▼▼▼▼▼▼▼▼▼▼▼▼▼▼▼▼▼▼▼▼▼▼▼▼▼▼▼▼▼▼▼▼▼▼▼

The U.S. Embassy and Consular Offices in Mexico provide a variety of services to U.S. citizens, including the replacement of lost passports, notifying people in emergencies, and assisting families when a U.S. citizen dies in Mexico. Registering your passport with the embassy is recommended and speeds the processing time if it is lost.

U.S. Embassy, Paseo de la Reforma 305, México, D. F. 06500. Telephone: 211-0042.

U.S. Consulates

U.S. Consulate General, Avenida López Mateos 924-N, **Ciudad Juárez, Chihuahua.** Telephone: 525-6066.

U.S. Consulate General, Progreso 175, **Guadalajara, Jalisco.** Telephone: 25-2998 or 25-2700.

U.S. Consulate General, Calle Monterrey 141, Poniente, **Hermosillo, Sonora.** Telephone: 723-75.

U.S. Consulate General, Avenida Primera No. 2002, **Matamoros, Tamaulipas.** Telephone: 2-52-50 or 2-52-51.

U.S. Consulate General, Circunvalación No. 120 Centro, **Mazatlán, Sinaloa.** Telephone: 5-2205.

U.S. Consulate General, Paseo Montejo 453, **Mérida, Yucatán.** Telephone: 25-5011.

U.S. Consulate General, Avenida Constitución 411 Poniente, **Monterrey, Nuevo León.** Telephone: 45-2120.

U.S. Consulate, Avenida Allende 3330, Colonia Jardín, **Nuevo Laredo, Tamaulipas.** Telephone: 4-0696 or 4-0512.

U.S. Consulate, Tapachula 96, **Tijuana, Baja California Norte.** Telephone: 681-7400 or 585-2000.

U.S. Consular Agents

Resident consular agents have been designated in other Mexican cities to help visitors and residents. The following is a listing of the agents' cities and telephone numbers:

- Acapulco: Telephone: 5-7207, extension 273.

- Puerto Vallarta: Telephone: 2-0069.

- San Miguel de Allende: Telephone: 2-2357.

About the Author

▼▼

Michael J. Zamba, a former journalist in Mexico, is the founder and editor of *México Today!*, a highly acclaimed quarterly carrying news and features for mature travelers to Mexico. Zamba's work has appeared in a variety of publications in the United States and Mexico, including the *Christian Science Monitor*, *Reader's Digest*, and the *Mexico City News*. A resident of Washington, D.C., Zamba continues to travel to and write about Mexico.

TRAVEL AND CULTURE BOOKS

"World at Its Best" Travel Series
Britain, France, Germany, Hawaii,
Holland, Hong Kong, Italy, Spain,
Switzerland, London, New York, Paris,
Washington, D.C., San Francisco

Passport's Travel Guides and References
IHT Guides to Business Travel in Asia &
Europe
Only in New York
Mystery Reader's Walking Guides:
London, England, New York, Chicago
Chicago's Best-Kept Secrets
London's Best-Kept Secrets
New York's Best-Kept Secrets
The Japan Encyclopedia
Japan Today!
Japan at Night
Japan Made Easy
Discovering Cultural Japan
Living in Mexico
The Hispanic Way
Guide to Ethnic Chicago
Guide to Ethnic London
Guide to Ethnic New York
Guide to Ethnic Montreal
Passport's Trip Planner & Travel Diary
Chinese Etiquette and Ethics in Business
Korean Etiquette and Ethics in Business
Japanese Etiquette and Ethics in Business
How to Do Business with the Japanese
Japanese Cultural Encounters
The Japanese

Passport's Regional Guides of France
Auvergne, Provence, Loire Valley,
Dordogne & Lot, Languedoc, Brittany, South
West France, Normandy & North West
France, Paris, Rhône Valley & Savoy,
France for the Gourmet Traveler

Passport's Regional Guides of Indonesia
New Guinea, Java, Borneo, Bali, East of
Bali, Sumatra, Spice Islands,
Sulawesi, Exploring the Islands of
Indonesia

Up-Close Guides
Paris, London, Manhattan, Amsterdam,
Rome

Passport's "Ticket To..." Series
Italy, Germany, France, Spain

**Passport's Guides: Asia, Africa, Latin
America, Europe, Middle East**
Japan, Korea, Malaysia, Singapore, Bali
Burma, Australia, New Zealand, Egyp
Kenya, Philippines, Portugal, Moscov
St. Petersburg, The Georgian Repub
Mexico, Vietnam, Iran, Berlin, Turke

Passport's China Guides
All China, Beijing, Fujian, Guilin,
Hangzhou & Zhejiang, Hong Kong,
Macau, Nanjing & Jiangsu, Shanghai
The Silk Road, Taiwan, Tibet, Xi'an,
The Yangzi River, Yunnan

Passport's India Guides
All India; Bombay & Goa; Dehli, Agra
& Jaipur; Burma; Pakistan;
Kathmandu Valley; Bhutan; Museum
of India; Hill Stations of India

Passport's Thai Guides
Bangkok, Phuket, Chiang Mai, Koh Su

On Your Own Series
Brazil, Israel

"Everything Under the Sun" Series
Spain, Barcelona, Toledo, Seville,
Marbella, Cordoba, Granada, Madri
Salamanca, Palma de Majorca

Passport's Travel Paks
Britain, France, Italy, Germany, Spain

Exploring Rural Europe Series
England & Wales, France, Greece,
Ireland, Italy, Spain, Austria,
Germany, Scotland, Ireland by Bicyc

Regional Guides of Italy
Florence & Tuscany, Naples & Campa
Umbria, the Marches & San Marino

Passport Maps
Europe, Britain, France, Italy, Holland
Belgium & Luxembourg, Scandinav
Spain & Portugal, Switzerland, Aust
& the Alps

Passport's Trip Planners & Guides
California, France, Greece, Italy

PASSPORT BOOKS
a division of *NTC Publishing Group*
Lincolnwood, Illinois USA